FIFA
WOMEN'S
WORLD CUP

AU 20
NZ 23 ™

Published in 2023 under licence by Welbeck, an imprint of Welbeck Non-Fiction Limited, part of the Welbeck Publishing Group.
Based in London and Sydney.

www.welbeckpublishing.com

ISBN 978-1-80279-630-8

10 9 8 7 6 5 4 3 2 1

Printed in Lithuania.

Editor: Conor Kilgallon
Design Manager: Russell Knowles
Design: Luke Griffin
Picture Research: Paul Langan
Production: Rachel Burgess

The facts and stats in this book are correct as of January 2023.

FIFA
WOMEN'S
WORLD CUP
AU·NZ·23™

THE OFFICIAL GUIDE

CATHERINE ETOE, JEN O'NEILL
& NATALIA SOLLOHUB

CONTENTS

*

© FIFA TM

INTRODUCTION

Every FIFA Women's World Cup is unique and this global showpiece is no exception. Predicted to be the greatest yet, it has already broken new ground with a series of memorable firsts. Now Australia and New Zealand are ready to stage the biggest women's sporting event on earth.

The FIFA Women's World Cup has come a long way since the very first tournament in China PR 32 years ago, when matches lasted just 80 minutes.

In 1999, the competition was expanded from 12 to 16 teams, with a new iconic trophy for the winners to hold aloft. At Canada 2015, a record 24 nations competed in the finals, the first to be played on artificial turf.

When Australia and New Zealand, called Aotearoa in Māori, were confirmed as hosts for the FIFA Women's World Cup 2023, it was clear that this ninth edition of the competition would be another step along the ladder of progress.

A binational tournament, with co-hosts from separate confederations, held in the southern hemisphere and featuring 32 teams, all for the very first time – new markers had been laid down before a ball had even been kicked.

The football will be of the highest standard, of that we can be sure. Yet it is not just the players competing on the pitch in Australia and New Zealand who can aspire to the tournament's ethos of "Beyond Greatness™".

"Sport changes lives, this World Cup will change lives," declared Australian Federal Minister for Sport, Anika Wells, at the draw in 2022.

At this moment in time and after all the challenges thrown up by the global pandemic, women's football really can inspire and transform the opportunities for girls and women in societies all around the world.

The tournament has also recognised the importance of the Indigenous cultures and people of Australia and Māori in New Zealand, and that is reflected in the imagery, language and place names being used. This sense of inclusion, equality and respect fits in many ways with the key values of both this particular FIFA Women's World Cup, and also the women's game itself.

Of course, there is no greater joy than winning and the USA, champions of the inaugural contest in 1991 and winners of further crowns in 1999, 2015 and 2019, return with one goal in mind – to become the first nation to make it three titles in a row.

Their task will be a supremely difficult one. Germany, the first back-to-back champions in the early to mid-2000s, have regrouped and rebuilt.

Canada have the gold medal won at the Tokyo Olympics two years ago in their locker, England are emboldened by European glory, Brazil and China PR likewise are queens of their confederations.

The 2011 champions Japan, one of the original 12 nations at the first-ever finals, are revitalised once more.

Norway, runners-up in 1991 and champions in 1995; the Netherlands, finalists in 2019; Sweden, silver medallists in 2003; France, Spain and others all have the talent and legitimate hopes of success too.

As investment, support and media coverage of women's football increase, so do the standard and level of competition across the world.

The old guard are returning but, as this year's debutants have proved, there are new stars emerging, new teams arriving, new dreams to be fulfilled and more memories to be made.

LEFT: Kate Taylor and Ava Collins at the FIFA Women's World Cup "One Year To Go" event.
RIGHT: Who will lift the FIFA Women's World Cup trophy this time?

< 8 >

WELCOME TO THE FIFA WOMEN'S WORLD CUP

*

This ninth edition of the FIFA Women's World Cup, and the first to be held in the Asia-Pacific region, has been eagerly anticipated and not without cause. Co-hosted by two great sporting nations in ten stadiums across nine beautiful cities, it will bring an unprecedented number of teams together, some of the biggest names, top sides and ambitious newcomers all battling to be crowned the best in the world.

ALL EYES ON AUSTRALIA & NEW ZEALAND

The FIFA Women's World Cup in Australia and New Zealand is set to be the biggest yet. Already groundbreaking with more teams than ever before, this tournament will also go down in history as the first to be co-hosted and the first to be held in the southern hemisphere.

"We did it!" tweeted the *Matildas'* talismanic striker Sam Kerr in June 2020 when Australia and New Zealand learnt they had been chosen to host the biggest women's football tournament on the planet.

Ahead of the announcement, images of the *Matildas* and *Football Ferns* had been transposed on to Sydney Opera House in a vibrant light show; Auckland's equally iconic Sky Tower had shone brightly in the colours of the joint "As One" bid campaign.

It had taken hard work to get to this point, the two confederations, teams, nations and governments coming together on a bid that promised not just a historic world-class football tournament, but a legacy beyond that.

After Brazil and Japan both withdrew, Colombia and the Antipodean neighbours were in the running for hosting rights and the wait on that June morning in 2020 to discover which had been chosen was agonising.

Once the words "Australia and New Zealand" had been uttered by FIFA President Gianni Infantino on his live broadcast from Zurich, however, the celebrations Down Under could begin.

"This will be a chance of a lifetime to connect with fans," said delighted New Zealand skipper Ali Riley. "We barely play any home games, because we are so far away from everywhere else, so this is epic."

The FIFA Council had voted 22 to 13 in favour of the Trans-Tasman "As One" bid and its offer of ideal playing conditions, state-of the-art venues in breathtaking cities and the creation of a legacy for the women's game in the Asia-Pacific region and beyond.

"This is about inspiring the next generation of girls, by leading the way on the field and off it," said Kerr. "We're ready to embrace the world and make you feel right at home too."

The qualified teams have already received an official Māori welcome with a *pōwhiri* in Auckland from Indigenous Māori tribe Ngāti Whātua Ōrākei.

With these two diverse nations home to a combined 200 cultures and 300 languages, every one of the 32 teams at these global finals can expect warm support wherever they go as well.

Adding to that "home away from home" feeling will be the

FIFA WOMEN'S WORLD CUP 2023™

The Member Associations of

AUSTRALIA, NEW ZEALAND (AS ONE BID)

...'s World Cup 2023™
...nner's Trophy

ABOVE: Fatma Samoura and Gianni Infantino of FIFA after the winning hosts' announcement.

< 12 >

ABOVE: An image of *Matildas* captain Sam Kerr performing her famous goal celebration is projected on to the Sydney Opera House.

competition's first-ever Team Base Camps, offering each national side a combined training site and accommodation.

Australia and New Zealand are, of course, no strangers to major sporting events, having hosted their fair share of blockbusters over the years. In 2000, Canberra, Melbourne and Sydney played host to the Women's Olympic Football Tournament, drawing 326,215 spectators. Around 1.5 million fans are expected to attend these finals, with about 2 billion more watching at home.

"This FIFA World Cup will not just be the best ever, it will turn your two countries upside down," FIFA President Infantino said at the draw in 2022.

An upsurge in interest in the *Matildas* was already in evidence, with a combined 56,604 fans turning out for their double-header series with reigning world champions USA in Sydney and Newcastle in late 2021.

China PR and the USA have twice previously hosted the global finals, while Sweden, Germany, Canada and France have all done so once.

They all helped advance the women's game, but France 2019 was groundbreaking, with 1.12 billion viewers tuning in on TV and digital platforms, while the USA v. Netherlands final was the most-watched women's match in history.

Among the stars then was *Matildas* captain Kerr, who scored five goals, four coming against Jamaica in the group stage before Australia fell in the round of 16 to Norway on penalties.

It was a disappointing end for the three-time quarter-finalists, who have been present at every finals since Sweden 1995 and were one of 12 teams in the 1988 International Women's Football Tournament, a trial event for the FIFA Women's World Cup.

New Zealand were among the 12 participants in the inaugural finals in 1991, but they have yet to win a match in five editions.

With their nations behind them in 2023, though, who knows what the *Football Ferns* and *Matildas* can achieve?

The competition will be fierce, but "Beyond Greatness" is the slogan of this FIFA Women's World Cup, in line with its aim to unite and inspire through the power of the tournament and women's football.

Regardless of who ultimately lifts the coveted trophy in Sydney, the women's game will surely be the winner in the end.

< 13 >

THE STADIUMS

———————— * ————————

Nine cities and ten stadiums will be awash with noise and colour as these two nations proudly showcase their state-of-the art sports facilities, culturally vibrant communities and stunning natural beauty. Four venues in New Zealand will host fixtures, including the opening match at Auckland's historic Eden Park, while five cities across Australia will provide the setting for all other games, culminating in the final at Sydney's spectacular Stadium Australia.

THE STADIUMS

The FIFA Women's World Cup will have ten stadiums across nine host cities. Australia has six stadiums located in Sydney, Adelaide, Brisbane, Melbourne and Perth. New Zealand has four stadiums in Auckland, Dunedin, Hamilton and Wellington.

EDEN PARK – A RICH HISTORY IN MAKING SPORTING MEMORIES

- **48,276 CAPACITY**
- **NEW ZEALAND'S NATIONAL STADIUM AND LARGEST "LIVE EXPERIENCE" VENUE**
- **THE OFFICIAL HOME OF AUCKLAND CRICKET AND AUCKLAND RUGBY UNION SINCE 1910 AND 1925, RESPECTIVELY**
- **CITY: AUCKLAND/TĀMAKI MAKAURAU**

Eden Park will host the prestigious tournament-opening fixture between New Zealand and Norway and it is sure to be an unforgettable occasion. A further eight games, including a quarter-final and semi-final, will also be played at New Zealand's national stadium.

The city of Auckland is based around two sizeable harbours and is sometimes referred to as the "City of Sails" due to the popularity of watersports. With over 1.6 million residents, comprised of a multicultural demographic, it is the most populous metropolitan area in New Zealand.

The stadium is situated just three kilometres from the centre, in the suburb of Kingsland, and easily accessible.

This will be the third major international women's sporting event held in the arena in two years. Marquee matches in the ICC Women's Cricket World Cup and the Rugby World Cup, including the *Black Ferns*' victory in the final, were played here in 2022.

< **16** >

SYDNEY FOOTBALL STADIUM – A MODERN, WORLD-CLASS STADIUM

- **42,512 CAPACITY**
- **COMPLETELY REBUILT STATE-OF-THE-ART VENUE**
- **SEATING FEATURES EYE-CATCHING ARTWORK BY INDIGENOUS ARTIST TONY ALBERT**
- **CITY: SYDNEY/GADIGAL**

Just a short distance away from the harbour city's central business district lies the state-of-the-art Sydney Football Stadium.

Originally built in 1988, back in 2000 the venue notably played host to the Women's Olympic Football Tournament final at the Sydney Olympic Games.

It was closed in 2019, reopening in August 2022 after a multimillion-dollar rebuild and it will welcome fans from across the globe for five group games and one round of 16 match during this FIFA Women's World Cup.

Group F sides France and Jamaica will be up first on the new pitch, which has already played host to the Matildas and Canada in a friendly in 2022.

That night offered a tantalising taste of things to come, with fireworks bursting into the air, lights pulsing along the many tiered stands and 26,997 fans making their voices heard.

DUNEDIN STADIUM – AN UNDER-COVER ENGINEERING MARVEL

- **28,744 CAPACITY**
- **NEW ZEALAND'S ONLY COVERED STADIUM**
- **PREVIOUSLY HOSTED THE FIFA U-20 WORLD CUP 2015**
- **CITY: DUNEDIN/ŌTEPOTI**

Known locally as "The Glasshouse", this magnificent venue on the east coast of New Zealand's South Island is the first covered stadium in the country and its largest indoor multipurpose arena.

Also considered to be the world's first permanently roofed stadium with a natural grass pitch, it was built as a replacement for the old Carisbrook Stadium and is a straightforward 20-minute walk from the city's bustling centre.

A remarkable feat of engineering, work on the stadium got underway in 2009 and it was officially opened in 2011 in time to host matches for that year's Rugby World Cup. Today it caters for a wide range of events.

FIFA Women's World Cup co-hosts the *Football Ferns* will get a chance to play here when they take on Switzerland, with former world champions Japan also among the teams set to compete under its spectacular roof.

< 17 >

MELBOURNE RECTANGULAR STADIUM – A WORLD-CLASS SPORTING INFRASTRUCTURE

- 30,052 CAPACITY
- THE NEW $267.5 MILLION VENUE WAS OPENED IN 2010
- A GEODESIC DOME ROOF DESIGN GIVES IT A "BUBBLE-LIKE" APPEARANCE
- CITY: MELBOURNE/NAARM

Melbourne Rectangular Stadium is situated on the banks of the Yarra River, close to the city centre. A stone's throw away from the iconic Melbourne Cricket Ground, the stadium is part of a precinct that boasts an almost unrivalled sporting infrastructure capable of hosting a number of elite events, including the Australian Open.

Superseding neighbouring Olympic Park Stadium as the city's home of rectangular sports, the new ground was opened in 2010. Its ultra-modern bioframe design allows uninterrupted views of the pitch and required 50 per cent less steel than a traditional structure of similar size. Thousands of LED lights adorn the outside of the stadium and can be programmed to stage visually stunning displays.

It is the home of Melbourne City and Melbourne Victory football clubs, plus rugby league's Melbourne Storm and rugby union's Melbourne Rebels.

WELLINGTON REGIONAL STADIUM – A WARM, WELLINGTON WELCOME AWAITS

- 39,000 CAPACITY
- UNOFFICIALLY REFERRED TO AS "THE CAKE TIN"
- OPENED IN JANUARY 2000 AND THE TURF WAS UPGRADED IN 2016
- CITY: WELLINGTON/TE WHANGANUI-A-TARA

New Zealand's capital city is situated at the southern end of the North Island. It is a vibrant and compact urban space.

Wellington Regional Stadium is a multipurpose arena set on the waterfront near to Wellington Central train station, where there is access to a 650-metre long elevated walkway. It has views of the harbour and takes less than ten minutes to travel its full length.

Due to its circular design, all seating within the stadium bowl is directed towards the centre of the pitch and has uninterrupted views, while the roof's engineering reduces the effect of the weather at pitch level.

The ground is also home to the country's only women's A-League side, Wellington Phoenix, and the men's team of the same name.

The highly anticipated group-stage rematch between FIFA Women's World Cup 2019 finalists the Netherlands and the USA will take place here.

< 18 >

WAIKATO STADIUM – A WELCOME RETURN TO HAMILTON

- 25,111 CAPACITY
- OPENED IN 1925 AS RUGBY PARK AND EXTENSIVELY REDEVELOPED
- LIES TO THE WEST OF THE SCENIC WAIKATO RIVER, THE LONGEST IN NEW ZEALAND
- CITY: HAMILTON/KIRIKIRIROA

Waikato Stadium will be familiar to anyone who attended the first-ever Play-Off Tournament for the FIFA Women's World Cup earlier this year, as well as those long-standing fans who were there for the U-17 edition in 2008.

Set to host five group games in this year's finals, this iconic stadium in the heart of New Zealand's fourth-largest city lies on the site of the old Rugby Park.

Its extensive redevelopment was completed in 2002 and it is a key venue for rugby as well as other sporting, cultural and music events, and exhibitions.

Its 50-metre tall lighting towers give the stadium a stylish appearance and there are carvings in its distinctive entrance and players' tunnel to mark the importance of Māori culture there.

Waikato also boasts a sustainable ethos, with a plethora of policies that include night-time turf watering and bicycle racks.

BRISBANE STADIUM – THE RIVER CITY IS READY FOR ACTION

- 52,263 CAPACITY
- ORIGINALLY KNOWN AS LANG PARK AND OPENED IN 1914, IT WAS REDEVELOPED 20 YEARS AGO
- THE HOME OF NATIONAL RUGBY LEAGUE SIDE BRISBANE BRONCOS
- CITY: BRISBANE/MEEANJIN

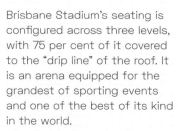

Brisbane Stadium's seating is configured across three levels, with 75 per cent of it covered to the "drip line" of the roof. It is an arena equipped for the grandest of sporting events and one of the best of its kind in the world.

Central to its redevelopment was traffic management.

Transport connections to the stadium are excellent and private car use is actively discouraged.

Public transport is free with a match ticket on game days on most rail and bus networks and services, and a 13-bay bus station can be found at the Milton Road end of the stadium.

In 1980, it hosted the first State of Origin game, the massively popular annual best-of-three rugby league series between Queensland and New South Wales, and has held significantly more games than any other venue.

A-League side Brisbane Roar plan a full-time return to their former home stadium soon.

< 19 >

PERTH RECTANGULAR STADIUM – A MODERN VENUE WITH HISTORIC FEATURES

- 22,225 CAPACITY
- MODERNISED AFTER A MULTI-MILLION DOLLAR UPGRADE
- HOME TO PERTH GLORY FC AND RUGBY UNION SIDE WESTERN FORCE
- CITY: PERTH/BOORLOO

Perth Rectangular Stadium, historically known as the Perth Oval, has undergone a multi-million dollar upgrade to be FIFA Women's World Cup ready.

Among the many improvements made to this historic venue are the installation of LED lighting, a new pitch and team bench areas, plus temporary infrastructure to cater for players, media and supporters.

Close to Perth's central business district, the ground has been redeveloped over the years, but it has been a site for sport for well over a century and is one of the community's much-loved landmarks and venues.

Its iconic north-west gates from its days as the Perth Oval are now heritage-listed.

During these finals, supporters of current Asian champions China PR and Olympic gold medallists Canada will be among those set to enjoy this stunning venue in five group matches.

HINDMARSH STADIUM – ALL ABOUT THE FOOTBALL

- 18,435 CAPACITY
- PURPOSE-BUILT FOR FOOTBALL AND HOME TO ADELAIDE UNITED
- ORIGINALLY BUILT IN 1960 AND REDEVELOPED FOR THE SYDNEY 2000 OLYMPIC GAMES
- CITY: ADELAIDE/TARNTANYA

Perhaps considered boutique compared to some of the other arenas being used in the tournament, Hindmarsh Stadium boasts the authenticity of being a truly football-centred venue with an intimate atmosphere.

It has hosted football matches since the 1960s and AFC Women's Asian Cup 2006 fixtures, as well as ties during the Sydney Games.

The main grandstand was upgraded in 2000 and the three terraces were replaced with all-new seating. A suite of further upgrades took place last year ready for the FIFA Women's World Cup 2023: the eastern grandstand is now covered, the playing surface relaid, contemporary turnstiles added, four new floodlights installed alongside two jumbo screens and an updated sound system.

Adelaide is the capital of South Australia and is world famous for the quality of the wine-producing regions nearby.

< 20 >

- 83,500 CAPACITY
- SCENE OF MANY SPORTING TRIUMPHS AND HISTORIC MOMENTS
- IMPRESSIVE VENUE SET TO HOST THE FIFA WOMEN'S WORLD CUP FINAL
- CITY: SYDNEY/GADIGAL

Stadium Australia will form the impressive backdrop to the *Matildas'* opening game and four of this year's FIFA Women's World Cup knockout matches, including the prestigious final.

Built for the Sydney Olympic and Paralympic Games, it has been the scene of many magical sporting moments over the years.

Body-suited Australian athlete Cathy Freeman was roared on to a 400m gold-medal triumph in this stadium back in 2000.

In 2021, more than 36,000 fans cheered on Australia against the USA in the same venue, setting a new attendance record for the *Matildas* on home soil.

Originally built to house 110,000 spectators, its capacity was reduced 20 years ago and it can host both rugby codes as well as football, Aussie Rules, American football and cricket.

A short walking distance from the nearest train station, the stadium was built with sustainability in mind, storing rainwater for use on the pitch and also using recycled water for flushing toilets.

< 21 >

ROAD TO THE FIFA WOMEN'S WORLD CUP

*

This first edition of the FIFA Women's World Cup with a newly expanded number of 32 teams offered more opportunities for nations from the six confederations to earn a prized place at Australia & New Zealand 2023. Players gave their all across varying qualifying formats, from competitive group stages spanning two seasons to one-off tournaments aligned with prestigious continental titles. There was even a newly introduced inter-confederation Play-Off Tournament for finals hopefuls.

QUALIFIERS: EUROPE

The road to Australia & New Zealand 2023 for the continent's finest began in earnest back in September 2021 when a record 51 nations kicked off in a hotly contested European qualifying competition.

By October 2022, after campaigns that had delivered unprecedented numbers of goals, some fine winning runs, tense finales and a thrilling play-off competition to determine the last two finalists, the 11 teams were decided. The FIFA Women's World Cup fate of three nations was settled as early as April 2022, when Sweden, Spain and France completed their campaigns with games to spare.

Ironically, the only match **Sweden** failed to gather all three points in was the 1-1 draw with the Republic of Ireland that maintained the *Blågult*'s ever-present status at the finals. Lina Hurtig and Fridolina Rolfö top-scored for Sweden with

five goals each in qualifying. Kosovare Asllani's second-half leveller against the Republic of Ireland in Gothenburg would seal their fate.

Spain had been untouchable in Group B and were all set for a third consecutive finals after a 2-0 win over Scotland in Glasgow, courtesy of two Jennifer Hermoso goals. *La Roja*'s smooth-as-you-like campaign saw them notch up eight wins out of eight, with a remarkable 53 scored and none conceded.

France made sure of their fifth finals appearance with two matches to go thanks to Delphine Cascarino's goal in a slender 1-0 win over Slovenia.

Wales had pushed them four days earlier, but they had survived to edge that tie 2-1 and their perfect campaign ended in September with victories over Estonia and Greece.

In May, it was **Denmark**'s turn to celebrate. Riding high in Group E, their lead was unassailable once Russia were suspended and their results annulled. The Danes went on to conclude their campaign without dropping a point, ending with a second 5-1 victory over Montenegro in September.

That month also saw past champions **Norway** qualify in their first match under former playing legend Hege Riise. Group runners-up Belgium took it to the wire, but Tuva Hansen's first international goal in an end-to-end 1-0 away win over the *Red Flames* in front of a record crowd settled matters in their penultimate qualifier.

Bronze medallists in 2015, **England** were through to their sixth finals with a game to spare, going on to top Group D with ten clean-sheet victories. Their tally of 80 goals was the highest in UEFA women's qualifying history. Beth Mead assisted on 12 of those and found the net herself 13 times, scoring three in England's biggest-ever win, 20-0 against Latvia.

A 3-0 win in Bursa saw two-time champions **Germany** maintain their ever-present

ABOVE: Delphine Cascarino's goal against Slovenia sent France to the FIFA Women's World Cup.

< 24 >

ABOVE: Ellen White became England's record goalscorer with a hat-trick in their 20-0 win over Latvia.

to Australia & New Zealand 2023. As the highest-ranked side, **Switzerland** went straight through to Round 2, and beat Wales 2-1 in Zurich to claim their second-ever finals place.

With just one defeat and two draws in Group A, the **Republic of Ireland** went through to Round 2 as one of the top three play-off teams. Standing in their way was a Scotland side that had beaten Austria days earlier. Ireland edged this one, with 'keeper Courtney Brosnan's penalty save and Amber Barrett's goal in the 72nd minute securing a 1-0 victory in front of more than 10,000 fans at Hampden Park.

The question then was whether Portugal could grab that 12th possible UEFA place at this year's finals via the inter-confederation play-offs. The third-best play-off side had seen off Belgium 2-1 and Iceland 4-1 in extra time, leaving them needing just one more win against either Cameroon or Thailand in February 2023 to make it.

status at the finals. Defeat to Serbia in April was the only blot on their copybook but, after seeing off Türkiye, they concluded with an 8-0 thumping of Bulgaria, in which Lea Schüller weighed in with a hat-trick to finish as Group H top scorer with 15 goals in nine games.

Just two points separated **Italy** from Group G rivals Switzerland ahead of their final qualifiers but goals from Valentina Giacinti and Lisa Boattin against Romania secured Italy's qualification.

The battle for Group C was a nail-biter. France 2019 finalists the **Netherlands** had overcome Iceland in Reykjavik and were otherwise unbeaten, but were twice held to draws by the Czech Republic. Iceland, on the other hand, had only dropped points to the Dutch, leading to a crunch final game in Utrecht. The Netherlands had to win, but appeared destined for the play-offs until Esmee Brugts' strike in time added on snatched a decisive

1-0 victory to break Icelandic hearts.

That left Iceland joining eight other runners-up in a play-off battle that would see two more teams progress directly

ABOVE: Republic of Ireland manager Vera Pauw and Denise O'Sullivan celebrate beating Scotland to qualify.

< 25 >

QUALIFIERS: REST OF THE WORLD

Surprises were sprung, new heroines came to the fore and fans turned out in record numbers in 2022 as nations across the five other confederations strived to stake their claim on a ticket to this year's finals.

Four proud newcomers and some of the biggest names in world football made the cut, with others pinning their hopes on success in the inter-confederation play-offs.

AFC

Five Asian nations were the first to reach this year's finals, with their places decided via the prestigious AFC Women's Asian Cup in early 2022. They endured strict pandemic precautions, played without fans and had seen hosts India sadly forced to withdraw after a COVID-19 outbreak in their camp. Even so, the 11 remaining teams, who included IR Iran for the first time, put on a show of flowing football, producing a few surprises along the way.

The **Philippines** made history, with a dramatic penalty shoot-out win over Chinese Taipei in the quarters, securing their first-ever appearance at a global finals.

Joining them were eventual champions **China PR** and runners-up **Korea Republic**, who had pulled off a shock win over title hopefuls Australia in the quarter-finals.

Japan had their ticket in the bag with a 7-0 last-eight win over Thailand, although they missed the chance to defend their title, losing to China PR in a semi-final penalty shoot-out.

Vietnam also made it through, beating Thailand 2-0 and Chinese Taipei 2-1 in repêchage for the fifth ticket on offer, while their opponents reached the inter-confederation Play-Off Tournament instead.

CAF

For the first time, four African teams booked automatic spots at this year's finals via the biennial CAF Women's Africa Cup of Nations in July 2022.

It had taken a two-stage qualifying process to whittle a record 45 competing nations – 20 more than in 2018 – down to the final 12.

Joining hosts Morocco were Cameroon, Nigeria, Senegal, South Africa, Tunisia, Uganda and Zambia, along with debutants Botswana, Burkina Faso, Burundi and Togo.

After a fiercely fought group stage and quarter-final victories, **Morocco** and **Zambia** had done enough to book their first-ever berth at the global finals.

South Africa topped their group ahead of reigning champions **Nigeria**, but both would return to the world stage with 1-0 last-eight wins over Tunisia and Cameroon respectively.

Cameroon and Senegal's journey was not at an end, however, with both sides winning repêchage matches to reach the inter-confederation play-offs.

ABOVE: Morocco's players are in dreamland after confirming their place at Australia & New Zealand 2023.

< 26 >

ABOVE: Tamires, Rafaelle and Debinha lift the *Copa América Femenina* trophy after Brazil's 2022 triumph.

Concacaf

A total of 30 teams entered the qualifying competition to reach the Concacaf W Championship, six group winners joining top-ranked Canada and the USA at the tournament in Mexico last summer.

Alongside the continental crown, four automatic spots and two play-off places for this year's global finals were at stake, with the eventual winner also heading to the 2024 Olympics.

After an emphatic victory over Trinidad & Tobago, **Canada** were assured of their FIFA Women's World Cup place when a Julia Grosso goal edged them past Panama.

Costa Rica would also beat those two sides to be sure of their return to the world stage.

Reigning world champions the **USA** were certain of a title defence after overcoming Haiti 3-0 and Jamaica 5-0. An Alex Morgan penalty would also see them beat Canada in the final to retain their Concacaf crown and reach the Olympics.

Jamaica bounced back from their loss to the USA to reach a historic second consecutive FIFA Women's World Cup. Their 4-0 victory over Haiti was enough after earlier beating Mexico.

Third in their groups, Haiti and Panama lived to fight another day, going through to the inter-confederation play-offs.

CONMEBOL

All ten South American member nations headed to Colombia in July 2022 for the ninth edition of the *Copa América Femenina*.

The tournament would determine qualification for the FIFA Women's World Cup 2023, providing three direct places and two play-off slots.

Colombia and **Brazil** won all four of their group games before beating Argentina 1-0 and Paraguay 2-0, respectively, to reach the tournament decider and book spots at Australia & New Zealand 2023.

While Pia Sundhage's Brazil side claimed the championship crown courtesy of a Debinha penalty in the final against Colombia, **Argentina** staged a second-half comeback to beat Paraguay 3-1 in the third-place match to clinch the final direct ticket.

That defeat sent Paraguay into the inter-confederation play-offs, alongside Chile, who had edged Venezuela on penalties in the battle for fifth place.

OFC

Nine Oceania Football Confederation teams, minus New Zealand and American Samoa, headed to Fiji in July for the 2022 OFC Women's Nations Cup. After finishing as runners-up three times, in 2007, 2010 and 2014, Papua New Guinea finally claimed the title by beating Fiji 2-1 and, as winners, advanced to the inter-confederation play-offs.

< 27 >

QUALIFYING RESULTS AND TABLES

While some teams have extended their streaks of never having missed a FIFA Women's World Cup, others have fullfilled their dreams of qualifying for the first time.

AFC (ASIA): 5 QUALIFIERS AND 2 INTERCONTINENTAL PLAY-OFF PLACES

AFC Women's Asian Cup

Group A:	P	W	D	L	GF	GA	Pts
China PR	2	2	0	0	11	0	6
Chinese Taipei	2	1	0	1	5	4	3
IR Iran	2	0	0	2	0	12	0

Group B:	P	W	D	L	GF	GA	Pts
Australia	3	3	0	0	24	1	9
Philippines	3	2	0	1	7	4	6
Thailand	3	1	0	2	5	3	3
Indonesia	3	0	0	3	0	28	0

Group C:	P	W	D	L	GF	GA	Pts
Japan	3	2	1	0	9	1	7
Korea Republic	3	2	1	0	6	1	7
Vietnam	3	0	1	2	2	8	1
Myanmar	3	0	1	2	2	9	1

Quarter-finals:			
Korea Republic	1-0	Australia
Japan	7-0	Thailand
China PR	3-1	Vietnam
Philippines	1-1 AET 4-3 pens	Chinese Taipei

Semi-finals:			
Korea Republic	2-0	Philippines
China PR	2-2 AET 4-3 pens	Japan

Final:			
China PR	3-2	Korea Republic

Repêchage play-off:			
Vietnam	2-0	Thailand
Chinese Taipei	3-0	Thailand
Vietnam	2-1	Chinese Taipei

ABOVE: Korea Republic's Choe Yu-ri opens the scoring in the AFC Women's Asian Cup final in 2022.

< 28 >

CAF (AFRICA): 4 QUALIFIERS AND 2 INTERCONTINENTAL PLAY-OFF PLACES

Women's Africa Cup of Nations

Group A:	P	W	D	L	GF	GA	Pts
Morocco	3	3	0	0	5	1	9
Senegal	3	2	0	1	3	1	6
Burkina Faso	3	0	1	2	2	4	1
Uganda	3	0	1	2	3	7	1

Group B:	P	W	D	L	GF	GA	Pts
Zambia	3	2	1	0	5	1	7
Cameroon	3	1	2	0	3	1	5
Tunisia	3	1	0	2	4	4	3
Togo	3	0	1	2	3	9	1

Group C:	P	W	D	L	GF	GA	Pts
South Africa	3	3	0	0	6	2	9
Nigeria	3	2	0	1	7	2	6
Botswana	3	1	0	2	4	5	3
Burundi	3	0	0	3	3	11	0

Quarter-finals:		
Zambia	1-1 AET 4-2 pens	Senegal
Morocco	2-1	Botswana
Nigeria	1-0	Cameroon
South Africa	1-0	Tunisia

Semi-finals:		
South Africa	1-0	Zambia
Morocco	1-1 AET 5-4 pens	Nigeria

Final:		
South Africa	2-1	Morocco

Third-place play-off:		
Zambia	1-0	Nigeria

Repêchage play-off:		
Senegal	0-0 4-2 pens	Tunisia
Cameroon	1-0	Botswana

Concacaf (NORTH, CENTRAL AMERICA AND CARIBBEAN):
4 QUALIFIERS AND 2 INTERCONTINENTAL PLAY-OFF PLACES

Concacaf W Championship

Group A:	P	W	D	L	GF	GA	Pts
USA	3	3	0	0	9	0	9
Jamaica	3	2	0	1	5	5	6
Haiti	3	1	0	2	3	7	3
Mexico	3	0	0	3	0	5	0

Group B:	P	W	D	L	GF	GA	Pts
Canada	3	3	0	0	9	0	9
Costa Rica	3	2	0	1	7	2	6
Panama	3	1	0	2	1	4	3
Trinidad & Tobago	3	0	0	3	0	11	0

Semi-finals:		
USA	3-0	Costa Rica
Canada	3-0	Jamaica

Final:		
USA	1-0	Canada

Third-place play-off:		
Jamaica	1-0 AET	Costa Rica

RIGHT: Alex Morgan celebrates her game-winning penalty against Canada in the 2022 Concacaf W Championship final.

< 29 >

CONMEBOL (SOUTH AMERICA): 3 QUALIFIERS AND 2 INTERCONTINENTAL PLAY-OFF PLACES

CONMEBOL *Copa América Femenina*

Group A:	P	W	D	L	GF	GA	Pts
Colombia	4	4	0	0	13	3	12
Paraguay	4	3	0	1	9	7	9
Chile	4	2	0	2	9	8	6
Ecuador	4	1	0	3	9	7	3
Bolivia	4	0	0	4	1	16	0

Group B:	P	W	D	L	GF	GA	Pts
Brazil	4	4	0	0	17	0	12
Argentina	4	3	0	1	10	4	9
Venezuela	4	2	0	2	3	5	6
Uruguay	4	1	0	3	6	9	3
Peru	4	0	0	4	0	18	0

Semi-finals:	Colombia	1-0	Argentina
	Brazil	2-0	Paraguay

Final:	Brazil	1-0	Colombia

Third-place play-off:	Argentina	3-1	Paraguay

Fifth-place play-off:	Chile	1-1 4-2 pens	Venezuela

OFC (OCEANIA): 1 INTERCONTINENTAL PLAY-OFF PLACE

OFC Women's Nations Cup

Group A:	P	W	D	L	GF	GA	Pts
Samoa	2	2	0	0	3	0	6
Cook Islands	2	0	1	1	1	2	1
Tonga	2	0	1	1	1	3	1

Group B:	P	W	D	L	GF	GA	Pts
Papua New Guinea	2	2	0	0	5	2	6
Tahiti	2	0	1	1	1	2	1
Vanuatu	2	0	1	1	1	3	1

Group C:	P	W	D	L	GF	GA	Pts
Fiji	2	1	1	0	4	2	4
Solomon Islands	2	0	2	0	3	3	2
New Caledonia	2	0	1	1	3	5	1

Quarter-finals:	Samoa	4-2	New Caledonia
	Papua New Guinea	3-3 AET 3-2 pens	Tonga
	Fiji	2-0	Cook Islands
	Solomon Islands	1-0	Tahiti

Semi-finals:	Papua New Guinea	3-0	Samoa
	Fiji	3-1	Solomon Islands

Final:	Papua New Guinea	2-1	Fiji

Third-place play-off:	Solomon Islands	1-1 6-5 pens	Samoa

RIGHT: Belgium's Tessa Wullaert (third from left) led the scoring charts in European qualifying with 17 goals.

< 30 >

UEFA (EUROPE): 11 QUALIFIERS AND 1 INTERCONTINENTAL PLAY-OFF PLACE

UEFA European Qualifying Competition

Group A:	P	W	D	L	GF	GA	Pts
Sweden	8	7	1	0	32	2	22
Republic of Ireland	8	5	2	1	26	4	17
Finland	8	3	1	4	14	12	10
Slovakia	8	2	2	4	9	9	8
Georgia	8	0	0	8	0	54	0

Group B:	P	W	D	L	GF	GA	Pts
Spain	8	8	0	0	53	0	24
Scotland	8	5	1	2	22	13	16
Ukraine	8	3	1	4	12	20	10
Hungary	8	3	0	5	19	19	9
Faroe Islands	8	0	0	8	2	56	0

Group C:	P	W	D	L	GF	GA	Pts
Netherlands	8	6	2	0	31	3	20
Iceland	8	6	0	2	25	3	18
Czech Republic	8	3	2	3	25	10	11
Belarus	8	2	1	5	7	26	7
Cyprus	8	0	1	7	2	48	1

Group D:	P	W	D	L	GF	GA	Pts
England	10	10	0	0	80	0	30
Austria	10	7	1	2	50	7	22
Northern Ireland	10	6	1	3	36	16	19
Luxembourg	10	3	0	7	9	45	9
North Macedonia	10	2	0	8	10	62	6
Latvia	10	1	0	9	8	63	3

Group E:	P	W	D	L	GF	GA	Pts
Denmark	8	8	0	0	40	2	24
Bosnia & Herzegovina	8	3	2	3	9	17	11
Montenegro	8	3	0	5	9	17	9
Azerbaijan	8	2	1	5	5	16	7
Malta	8	2	1	5	6	17	7

Group F:	P	W	D	L	GF	GA	Pts
Norway	10	9	1	0	47	2	28
Belgium	10	7	1	2	56	7	22
Poland	10	6	2	2	28	9	20
Albania	10	3	1	6	14	30	10
Kosovo	10	2	1	7	8	35	7
Armenia	10	0	0	10	1	71	0

Group G:	P	W	D	L	GF	GA	Pts
Italy	10	9	0	1	40	2	27
Switzerland	10	8	1	1	44	4	25
Romania	10	6	1	3	21	11	19
Croatia	10	3	1	6	6	18	10
Lithuania	10	1	2	7	7	35	5
Moldova	10	0	1	9	1	49	1

Group H:	P	W	D	L	GF	GA	Pts
Germany	10	9	0	1	47	5	27
Portugal	10	7	1	2	26	9	22
Serbia	10	7	0	3	26	14	21
Türkiye	10	3	1	6	9	26	10
Israel	10	3	0	7	7	25	9
Bulgaria	10	0	0	10	1	37	0

Group I:	P	W	D	L	GF	GA	Pts
France	10	10	0	0	54	4	30
Wales	10	6	2	2	22	5	20
Slovenia	10	5	3	2	21	6	18
Greece	10	4	1	5	12	28	13
Estonia	10	2	0	8	7	43	6
Kazakhstan	10	0	0	10	4	34	0

European play-off round 1:		
Scotland	1-0 AET	Austria
Wales	1-0 AET	Bosnia & Herzegovina
Portugal	2-1	Belgium

European play-off round 2:		
Portugal	4-1 AET	Iceland
Scotland	0-1	Republic of Ireland
Switzerland	2-1 AET	Wales

Inter-confederation Play-Off Tournament

Group A:		
Cameroon	v	Thailand
Portugal	v	Cameroon/Thailand

Group B:		
Senegal	v	Haiti
Chile	v	Senegal/Haiti

Group C:		
Chinese Taipei	v	Paraguay
Papua New Guinea	v	Panama
Chinese Taipei/Paraguay	v	Papua New Guinea/Panama

< 31 >

THE DRAW

The Aotea Centre on 22 October 2022 was the setting for the final and most important piece in the FIFA Women's World Cup 2023 jigsaw. Around 800 local and international guests gathered for the ceremony in Auckland amidst great excitement and anticipation.

As well as dignitaries such as the FIFA President and Secretary General, former New Zealand Prime Minister Jacinda Ardern and Australian Federal Minister for Sport Anika Wells, attendees included coaches and delegations from the 29 qualifiers – with the ten inter-confederation play-off hopefuls likewise watching on keenly – all eager to learn their team's fate.

Ahead of the formalities of the draw procedure, co-hosts Australia and New Zealand greeted those present, and a global audience following on TV and on FIFA+ online, with a fantastic display of Māori and First Nations culture. It was

followed by an irresistible video montage of the beautiful and dynamic cities that will welcome the teams and supporters.

With the mood around the auditorium buzzing, the former coach of the USA, Jill Ellis, entered the stage clutching the trophy her team had lifted in 2015 and 2019. Smiling, she whetted the appetite further as she looked ahead to July and August's tournament: "It is not only going to be the best, it will be the most competitive World Cup we have seen in our history."

Two-time FIFA Women's World Cup winner Carli Lloyd and sports presenter Amanda Davies conducted the draw, while a

duo of women's football greats, former *Matilda* Julie Dolan and ex-*Football Fern* Maia Jackman, and four men's FIFA Legends were among those performing the role of Draw Assistants.

With the match schedule and venues already confirmed, the 32 contenders were to be divided into eight groups of four. Co-hosts New Zealand and Australia and the six top-ranked teams – namely the USA, Sweden, Germany, England, France and Spain – filled Pot 1, while the remaining teams were allocated to Pots 2-4 based on October's FIFA/Coca-Cola Women's World Ranking. Also, FIFA convention is to keep members of

ABOVE: A captivating performance representing Māori and First Nations culture at the FIFA Women's World Cup 2023 draw.

< 32 >

ABOVE: The FIFA Women's World Cup 2023 draw at the Aotea Centre in Auckland.

the same qualifying zone apart in the group phase of finals, aside from UEFA teams where there are necessary exceptions.

With New Zealand's place in Group A pre-determined, one of the headline grabbers is their tournament-opening match at Eden Park on 20 July against former champions Norway.

Australia, meanwhile, already placed directly into pole position in Group B, will entertain debutants Republic of Ireland in Sydney later the same day. The *Matildas* also have Olympic champions Canada to contend with, though the two heavyweights of the group will hope to have done enough by the time they meet on 31 July.

An expanded tournament means fewer repeat groupings of sides that have become overfamiliar in the past – USA and Sweden, for example, have been drawn together six times previously – but there will be a mouth-watering rematch of the 2019 final between the USA and the Netherlands in Group E on 27 July. Firstly, though, holders USA are the daunting opponents for first-timers Vietnam, in Auckland, on 22 July.

Elsewhere, Group D features two continental champions in England and China PR, teams that conquered Europe and Asia in 2022, while in Group H North Africa's flagship side Morocco kick off their maiden finals with the prospect of facing two-time winners, and one of the potential favourites, Germany.

The draw ceremony was also the first public outing for the tournament's mascot Tazuni™, who is a fun, football-loving teenage penguin. Her name derives from a coming together of the words for her home – the Tasman Sea – and the theme of "unity", which is a core value of the competition. She is based on the Eudyptula minor species of bird which is native to New Zealand and Australia. Tazuni will be a likeable and recognisable figure for the event, both in imagery and when out and about promoting games and meeting the fans.

One admirer who has met her already is FIFA's Chief Women's Football Officer, Sarai Bareman: "Like millions of youngsters worldwide, football is how Tazuni expresses herself, and the FIFA Women's World Cup Australia & New Zealand 2023 will provide inspiration for a new generation of football fans and participants from across the globe."

All of the razzmatazz and the logistics aside, the purpose of the event was to seal the format for the greatest women's sporting event on earth – 32 teams will be striving to claim the ultimate prize on 20 August 2023.

RIGHT: Tazuni, the official mascot of the FIFA Women's World Cup 2023.

< 33 >

MEET
THE TEAMS

---

 *

For some debutant players heading to Australia and
New Zealand, simply making it to the FIFA Women's
World Cup 2023 will be a dream come true. They
will do their utmost to make their countries and
supporters proud, while other teams will have greater
ambitions. All previous winners of the coveted trophy
are returning but the international game is developing
apace — will a new nation rise to the occasion and
claim the global crown?

NEW ZEALAND

As the first joint-hosts of the competition, the *Football Ferns* will hope that home support spurs them on to record their first-ever victory at the FIFA Women's World Cup. This is their sixth appearance on this stage and the pressure and desire to succeed have never been greater.

COACH
JITKA KLIMKOVÁ

This former Czech Republic defender ended her top-flight club career at 1. FC Slovácko, becoming their coach for seven seasons while also working with the Czech U-19s. Gained her UEFA Pro Licence in 2008 and won the Australian W-League title and coach of the year award with Canberra United after joining in 2011. Started working with New Zealand's youth programme in 2013 before moving on to the USA in 2015. Led a *Young Football Ferns* side at the FIFA U-17 Women's World Cup 2014 and the USA at the 2018 U-20 edition. In 2013 she said: "It was always my dream to take a national team to a World Cup." A funny and passionate coach, her contract runs until 2027.

New Zealand are the dominant force in Oceania – an unchallenged position following Australia's switch to the Asian confederation in 2006 – and have appeared at every global finals since 2007.

Past OFC Nations Cup tournaments have seen them regularly win games against island nations with scorelines into double figures, so bypassing a qualifying competition as hosts for these finals will not have adversely affected their preparation.

On the contrary, their fixtures in the build-up to this tournament have featured plenty of important learning opportunities against top ten-ranked sides including Sweden and the USA, and

confidence-boosting results over fellow Australia & New Zealand 2023-bound nations.

Historically, the *Ferns* have been competitive at FIFA Women's World Cups – they have not conceded more than two goals in a game in the last three editions – but scoring against elite opponents has been where the struggle lies.

Two draws at Canada 2015 was the closest they have come to progressing to the knockout stage, including a 0-0 draw with the hosts. Disappointingly, four years later in France they were beaten in all three games, and the only time they registered on the scoresheet was through an own goal in the 2-1 loss to Cameroon.

Vastly experienced coach Tom

ABOVE: New Zealand will open the tournament at Eden Park, their national stadium.

Sermanni ended his term in charge after the Tokyo Games, where they again finished pointless in an extremely tough group including Australia, the USA and Sweden.

His replacement, Jitka Klimková, wants to change the narrative and for her women's programme to be bold and positive: "Whoever we are up against, New Zealand will be a team that plays to win."

It wasn't the smoothest of starts for Klimková. Pandemic-enforced border restrictions meant her new role required an extended period of remote working from her homeland, the Czech Republic.

Their coach may have been itching to get into the country but, ironically, for many years a diaspora of players have been heading in the opposite direction, out of New Zealand, for more competitive action and paid playing opportunities. In recent squads, only around a quarter of players called up have been home-based, with the rest playing in nearby Australia, or the USA, Scotland, England and Scandinavia. More talent could be persuaded to stay in future, though, now that Wellington Phoenix have entered Australia's professional A-League.

Centurion midfielder Betsy Hassett and forward Emma Rolston signed in 2022 for the start of the club's second season and key members of the historic bronze medal-winning team at the FIFA U-17 Women's World Cup 2018 are being nurtured there too. They include defenders Marisa van der Meer and Mackenzie Barry and forward Grace Wisnewski – who bagged both goals in their third-place 2-1 defeat of Canada.

The *Ferns* have genuine quality and experience in their squad. Defender Ali Riley and defensive midfielder Katie Bowen have

ALI RILEY
BORN: 30 OCTOBER 1987
POSITION: DEFENDER

Born in California, with a Kiwi father, the dependable and athletic full-back's impressive CV includes a number of top clubs in the USA and Sweden, with shorter stints in England and Germany. Her extended spell with FC Rosengård, between 2012 and 2018, brought her three *Damallsvenskan* titles and plenty of UEFA Women's Champions League experience. She made her international debut in February 2007 and has gone on to play every minute at four FIFA Women's World Cups and four Olympic Games. She is one of the team's most capped players, their upbeat leader and captain since 2017.

OLIVIA CHANCE
BORN: 5 OCTOBER 1993
POSITION: MIDFIELDER/ FORWARD

A quick, clever, left-footed player, she often provides the killer pass for her team's goals. Made headlines at 16 when she hit a hat-trick to help Claudelands Rovers win New Zealand's cup competition. Gained a finance degree in the USA and was her team's top scorer for three out of four seasons with the South Florida Bulls. Injury hampered her two years at Everton before figuring in every *Ferns* game at France 2019. After seasons with Bristol City, Brisbane Roar and her first Olympics, she signed for Celtic, winning the Scottish FA and League Cups in her first season.

several distinguished seasons in the National Women's Soccer League under their belts.

Klimková needs players to stay healthy. Most-capped Kiwi Ria Percival and her fellow midfielder Annalie Longo suffered ACL injuries last year and other regulars have had ongoing niggles. One uplifting development was seeing defender Rebekah Stott make her return a year after being diagnosed with Hodgkin's lymphoma.

Two matches in Christchurch in November 2022 ended an astonishing four-year spell without a fixture in their homeland. The

Ferns and their fans have been patient. If they get that first win, and more, it will be worth the wait.

WOMEN'S WORLD CUP RECORD

1991	Group stage (4th)
1995	Did not qualify
1999	Did not qualify
2003	Did not qualify
2007	Group stage (4th)
2011	Group stage (4th)
2015	Group stage (4th)
2019	Group stage (4th)

< 37 >

⊕ NORWAY

Norway boast a full set of silverware having won FIFA Women's World Cup, European and Olympic gold. The last of those was delivered 23 years ago. Now, a talented group under inspirational leadership are looking not to the past, but to a bright new future.

COACH
HEGE RIISE

Norway's record caps holder with 188 and scorer of 58 international goals, with FIFA Women's World Cup, European Championship and Olympic gold in her locker. Named Golden Ball as the best player at the FIFA Women's World Cup 1995, where she and team-mate Heidi Støre invented the iconic "snake" goal celebration. Played in Norway, Japan and the USA. Pia Sundhage's assistant with runners-up USA at the FIFA Women's World Cup 2011, she also won multiple titles as coach at LSK Kvinner and led Team GB at the Tokyo Games. In 2022, she steered Norway's U-19s to EURO silver. Humble, witty and determined, the 54-year-old says she enjoys bringing out the best in her players.

Norway had everything to play for when they walked out to face Belgium in Leuven in September 2022 for their penultimate FIFA Women's World Cup qualifier. A high-scoring win would put the *Red Flames* in the driving seat for the run-in; a victory would see Norway grab an automatic berth at this year's finals.

As a member of the side that had made it to the round of 16 in 2015 and captain of the group that reached the last eight at France 2019, Maren Mjelde knew exactly what was at stake.

"There is nothing cooler than playing at a World Cup," the skipper declared in the team huddle before kick-off. "And we can make that happen today, come on!"

Norway had endured a crushing early exit at the UEFA Women's EURO 2022 just weeks earlier and eight of the first XI from their last match then would start in Belgium. In that maiden outing under new head coach Hege Riise, pride was restored – defender Tuva Hansen whipping in a crucial winner to stun a record crowd of 7,636.

Norway had maintained their status as one of the FIFA Women's World Cup's ever-presents and closed out

ABOVE: This Norway side is ready to follow in the footsteps of giants.

< 38 >

qualifying unbeaten four days later with a 5-0 win over Albania in Oslo.

The smiles that greeted their achievement were in stark contrast to the tears that flowed at last summer's EURO after a humbling 8-0 defeat at the hands of eventual winners England, followed by a 1-0 loss to Austria.

Their sole victory, a 4-1 win over debutants Northern Ireland and their best start to a UEFA Women's EURO for over 20 years, was scant consolation for a nation that were European champions in 1987 and 1993 and losing finalists as recently as 2013.

In the wake of a second EURO group-stage exit on the bounce, however, their head coach for the past six years, Martin Sjögren, resigned.

By early August, fresh from leading the U-19s to European silver, legendary former midfielder Riise had taken the top job. With fellow 2000 Olympic Games gold medallist Monica Knudsen, and former national-team skipper Ingvild Stensland joining as assistants, a new era was underway.

With the potential banana skin of FIFA Women's World Cup qualifiers over, Norway would embark on a string of high-profile friendlies as preparation for Australia & New Zealand 2023. "Being able to meet the presumed best, and try out what we are working on, is important to us," Riise said.

A reminder of the very best of Norway's past, but a coach who could lead them to a new future, Riise had used her second match to blood promising U-23s including 2021 Toppserien player of the year, Marit Bratberg Lund, plus Mathilde Hauge Harviken and Sara Hørte.

GURO REITEN
BORN: 26 JULY 1994
POSITION: MIDFIELDER

All-action left-footer and fans' favourite with her work-rate, intelligence and goals. Won league titles under Hege Riise at LSK Kvinner, as well as back-to-back *Toppserien* top-scorer and best player awards. Also won goal of the year in 2018 and bagged 60 in 62 matches at LSK before switching to English Women's Super League side Chelsea in 2019. Has played on the wing, up front and wing-back for the *Blues* and made the PFA WSL Team of the Year in 2022. Debuted for Norway in 2014 and played her part in the run to the last eight at France 2019.

VILDE BØE RISA
BORN: 13 JULY 1995
POSITION: MIDFIELDER

Pacy, visionary playmaker who debuted for the national team in 2016 and reached a half-century of caps in June 2022. Missed EURO 2017 with an ACL injury but worked her way back to start every game at France 2019. Won the *Damallsvenskan* with Kopparbergs/Göteborg in 2020, also gaining UEFA Women's Champions League experience. Signed for the club she supported as a child, English outfit Manchester United, in 2021, going on to impress with her energy, positioning and goal threat. Was coached to the age of 14 by her late father Terje, who played for SK Brann.

With Riise and her assistant, the former U-23 coach Stensland, familiar with the potential across the age groups, there is every likelihood others will get a chance too.

As for Norway's core, with players like Mjelde, Ada Hegerberg, Ingrid Engen and Julie Blakstad to choose from, there is no doubt that it is packed with talent, with most of their big names playing high-quality opposition week-in, week-out at top clubs across Europe.

With Norwegian FA president Lise Klaveness working to give the national team everything they need to succeed too, Norway could once again be a force to be reckoned with.

WOMEN'S WORLD CUP RECORD

1991	Runners-up
1995	Winners
1999	Fourth place
2003	Quarter-finalists
2007	Fourth place
2011	Group stage (3rd)
2015	Round of 16
2019	Quarter-finalists

< 39 >

GROUP

A

PHILIPPINES

The Philippines Football Federation (PFF) was founded over a century ago in 1907. No Filipino team has ever come close to qualifying for a tournament on the global stage, until the women's side's astonishing achievement at the start of 2022.

COACH
ALEN STAJCIC

Former schoolboy international and New South Wales Premier League player, "Staj" says steering the *Filipinas* to the global showpiece event was probably the best experience in his 20-year coaching career. His journey includes the NSW Institute of Sport women's football programme, the *Young Matildas* and Sydney FC (2008-2014) where he claimed two W-League championship wins. As head coach, he led Australia to the last eight at Canada 2015 and Rio 2016 and was shortlisted for The Best FIFA Women's Coach in 2018. Stajcic was sacked shortly before France 2019 following an internal review into the team's culture, but subsequently reached a financial settlement. Worked in the men's club game in Australia before answering the call from the Philippines.

The success of the *Filipinas* (who switched their moniker from *Malditas* after their FIFA Women's World Cup qualification) is by far the biggest football-related news story in a nation that favours basketball, volleyball and boxing over the beautiful game.

Making the final four of the AFC Women's Asian Cup 2022 to earn a direct pass to Australia & New Zealand 2023 marked a meteoric rise for the team then ranked 13th in Asia.

In 2018, during their first appearance at the continental championship in 15 years, they had hoped to earn a place at France 2019 only to suffer a comprehensive 5-0 defeat to Korea Republic in the fifth-place match, which served as a play-off for the FIFA Women's World Cup.

These rewards have not come entirely overnight, however. Scouting for talent from the Filipino diaspora started around a decade ago. Only six of the 23-player squad for the 2022 Asian Cup were based in the Philippines. Twelve were playing in the USA, three in Europe, while two were active in Japan's WE League.

Prior to the tournament, former Australia coach Alen Stajcic – brought in at the end of October 2021 – had taken his squad on a two-month training camp in California. It proved vital both as a "getting to know you" exercise and as physical preparation,

ABOVE: The Philippines are Southeast Asian champions but FIFA Women's World Cup first-timers.

< 40 >

given they had played just two Asian Cup qualifiers between December 2019 and January 2022.

With two seasons of the amateur PFF Women's League, first introduced in 2016, cancelled due to the pandemic, some players had not kicked a ball competitively for 12 to 18 months.

Despite hurdles such as COVID-19 cases to overcome, under Stajcic and his staff, the powerfully motivated group were galvanised and bought into the challenge.

They showed they meant business in India when Chandler McDaniel's 81st-minute goal in their group opener earned them a 1-0 win, a first-ever against Thailand in 13 attempts.

After a scoreless first half, they lost to Australia 4-0, but bounced back to defeat Indonesia 6-0. They were now just one victory away from the dream ticket.

Quinley Quezada's goal in the quarter-final was cancelled out by Chinese Taipei's exquisite equaliser and, with extra time a stalemate, a pulsating shoot-out ensued and a new heroine emerged. With her team trailing 3-2, goalkeeper Olivia McDaniel, with only four caps to her name, saved two spot kicks either side of stepping up and scoring her own. Striker Sarina Bolden slotted in the decisive penalty in sudden death and the jubilant celebrations began. Losing 2-0 to Korea Republic in the semi-final did little to dampen the spirits.

Congratulatory messages flooded in from dignitaries and the glitterati, including the country's president as well as boxing-megastar-turned-politician, Manny Pacquiao.

Since then they have become "Queens" of Southeast Asia after winning the 2022 AFF

OLIVIA MCDANIEL
BORN: 14 OCTOBER 1997
POSITION: GOALKEEPER

American-born from a soccer-obsessed family with four brothers and a sister, McDaniel switched from playing up front to between the posts on the suggestion of her dad, a coach. Grew up idolising former USA goalkeeper Hope Solo. First trained with the Philippines national team at a camp in California as a schoolgirl. Younger sister Chandler is a star forward for the *Filipinas*. Both are also Milwaukee Panthers alumni. Shot to fame and into national sporting folklore by saving twice and scoring in the shoot-out that led to their historic qualification for this year's finals.

SARINA BOLDEN
BORN: 30 JUNE 1996
POSITION: FORWARD

Strong-running forward and vocal leader, and so often the provider of vital goals. The California native made her international debut while also enjoying a successful college soccer career at Loyola Marymount University. Attended a USA U-23s training camp before joining the *Filipinas*. Scored on her debut in a 2-1 win over Jordan at the 2018 AFC Women's Asian Cup. Netted the decisive penalty in the 2022 quarter-final shoot-out. Played in the inaugural season of Japan's professional WE League in 2021-22 with Chifure AS Elfen Saitama. The fans sing a song for her to the tune of "Can't Take My Eyes Off You".

Women's Championship on home soil, beating Thailand 3-0 in the final in front of 8,257 noisy fans. It was the nation's first-ever football title and created a further upsurge in TV ratings and public interest.

The team's preparations have also included friendly matches against sides from other confederations, like the Republic of Ireland, New Zealand and Costa Rica, as they seek to familiarise themselves with different playing styles.

No matter what transpires on the pitch at Australia & New Zealand 2023, the achievements of the *Filipinas* in 2022 have already inspired a nation.

WOMEN'S WORLD CUP RECORD

No Philippines team of any gender or any age has appeared on the global stage before, but this team did it in dramatic fashion by beating Chinese Taipei in a penalty shoot-out in the quarter-finals of the AFC Women's Asian Cup.

< 41 >

⊕ SWITZERLAND

Die Nati left it agonisingly late in their play–off tie to clinch qualification for these finals. They will be looking to get off to a quick and positive start in their second appearance at the FIFA Women's World Cup.

COACH
INKA GRINGS

Enjoyed a stellar career as a striker, netting 64 goals in 96 caps and three German player of the year accolades. During 16 years with FCR 2001 Duisburg, she bagged 353 goals in 271 games, was league top scorer six times and clinched the 2009 UEFA Women's Cup. Further honours came with FC Zurich in Switzerland and she also played in the USA. Featured at two FIFA Women's World Cups, claimed Olympic bronze in 2000 and won the UEFA Women's EURO as top scorer in 2005 and 2009. Debuted in the technical area at MSV Duisburg before coaching men's youth and lower-league sides in Germany. Rejoined FC Zurich in 2021, leading them to the title before switching to Switzerland at the start of this year.

Outgoing Switzerland coach Nils Nielsen was sporting a "Lion King" T-shirt under his jacket for the crunch round 2 play-off against Wales in Zurich. He said it symbolised the "fighting spirit" of his players and they certainly showed their battling qualities in a dramatic 2-1 comeback victory that booked *Die Nati*'s place at Australia & New Zealand 2023 and also marked a perfect sign-off as his contract reached its end.

Ramona Bachmann, so often the source of brilliance in the Swiss side, fired in a smart equaliser on the stroke of half-time but her team missed a penalty as they laboured to find another breakthrough. A shoot-out seemed inevitable until substitute Fabienne Humm's deft, near-post finish won the match in the 121st minute.

Die Nati had been consigned to second place in their qualifying group, and therefore into the play-offs, after dropping five costly points in two matches in April 2022 – a 1-1 draw in Romania followed by a 1-0 home defeat to Italy four days later, which cancelled out their brilliant 2-1 result in Palermo a few months earlier.

Relatively early advocates of modern women's football, Switzerland formed a women's league in 1970 and the first international took place in 1972. They have never been ranked lower than 31st in the world yet

ABOVE: Switzerland qualified with a last-gasp winner in the European play-offs.

< 42 >

missed out on six occasions before making it to their maiden FIFA Women's World Cup in 2015, and it took 11 attempts before they made it to their first European Championship in 2017.

Credit for the groundwork behind their progress goes to ex-Switzerland international Béatrice von Siebenthal and former head coach Martina Voss-Tecklenburg.

Von Siebenthal, coach of the senior and youth sides from 2005 to 2012, formed the national women's football academy; her successor from 2012 to 2018 and current Germany boss, Voss-Tecklenburg, transformed the team's mentality and guided them to their first major finals.

Former Denmark manager Nielsen took over in December 2018 and cultivated another shift in mindset, encouraging creativity and not fearing mistakes, an approach which has been tested at the sharp end of recent qualifying campaigns.

Having lost to the Netherlands in the European play-off final and failing to make it to France 2019, they secured a slot at UEFA Women's EURO 2022 via a two-legged play-off with the Czech Republic and a nail-biting penalty shoot-out.

A squad comprising talent from across the Swiss Women's Super League – the top-flight competition was revamped and relaunched in 2020 – and England, France, Germany and Spain, headed to the continental championship full of positivity.

However, a 2-2 draw with Portugal, the misfortune of a stomach bug that affected eight of the squad mid-tournament, then 2-1 and 4-1 losses to Sweden and the Netherlands, respectively, would not be enough to progress.

Die Nati have a better record in their one outing at the global finals. At Canada 2015 they chalked up a

LIA WÄLTI
BORN: 19 APRIL 1993
POSITION: MIDFIELDER

Captain, on-field organiser and calming, caring cornerstone of the team. She began her senior career at Young Boys, winning the league in 2010-11, then spent five seasons in Germany with 1. FFC Turbine Potsdam. After moving to Arsenal, she won the English Women's Super League 2018-19 title and made the PFA team of the year in her first season. She despatched her EURO 2022 qualifying play-off shoot-out penalty so coolly that it went viral and she earned her 100th cap in Switzerland's opener against Portugal at that tournament. She is studying for a degree in business administration and sports management.

ANA-MARIA CRNOGORČEVIĆ
BORN: 3 OCTOBER 1990
POSITION: DEFENDER/ FORWARD

Switzerland's all-time record caps holder and leading scorer, male or female. She has Croatian parents, dual nationality and grew up speaking Croatian at home. After spending almost a decade in Germany, predominantly with 1. FFC Frankfurt, then two seasons with Portland Thorns in the USA, she switched to Spain. A two-time UEFA Women's Champions League winner, whether operating as a winger, a forward or at right-back, she has excellent endurance and the bigger the game, the better she performs.

sizeable 10-1 victory over Ecuador in between going down 1-0 to Japan and 2-1 to Cameroon.

It was enough to progress to the knockout round as one of the top four third-place finishers, where they were edged 1-0 in the round of 16 by hosts Canada in front of a fervent crowd of over 53,000.

A handful of Die Nati are still amateurs, although they also boast experienced professionals like Gaëlle Thalmann, Noelle Maritz, Eseosa Aigbogun, Lia Wälti, Ana-Maria Crnogorčević, plus exciting younger stars Géraldine Reuteler and Svenja Fölmli.

Can they surpass their efforts of eight years ago, when they almost reached the last eight?

WOMEN'S WORLD CUP RECORD

1991	Did not qualify
1995	Did not qualify
1999	Did not qualify
2003	Did not qualify
2007	Did not qualify
2011	Did not qualify
2015	Round of 16
2019	Did not qualify

🇦🇺 AUSTRALIA

Australia hit new heights in 2021 with a fourth-place finish at the Olympic Games, their highest yet. Now, the *Matildas* are aiming to transfer that major tournament experience to this world stage as they look to make history at home.

COACH
TONY GUSTAVSSON

A charismatic, energetic coach with a raft of tournament experience. Assisted Pia Sundhage to win Olympic gold with the USA, following up with back-to-back FIFA Women's World Cup titles as No. 2 to Jill Ellis. In between, he led Swedish outfit Tyresö to the *Damallsvenskan* title and a UEFA Women's Champions League runners-up spot. A qualified maths and PE teacher, he kicked off his coaching career as player-manager with Swedish team Ytterhogdals IK in 2000, going on to coach several men's professional teams in Norway and his homeland. Switched to the women's game after compatriot Sundhage emailed to ask him to become her assistant; says she taught him the value of not taking yourself too seriously. Joined the *Matildas* from Hammarby in 2020.

Australia's players wept, leapt and hollered with joy when the news came through that they were to co-host this year's showpiece finals.

After that dream high, though, came the focus on preparation and one of the first items on the agenda for the *Matildas* was the need for a new leader. Popular coach Ante Milicic had delivered Olympic qualification but, with a pre-existing contract to honour, he would not lead them at the delayed tournament.

That task would fall to Swede Tony Gustavsson, who revealed a grand ambition when he was unveiled as new head coach in September 2020.

"We're going to create a legacy that no one could ever expect and a legacy that is bigger than ourselves," he said. The road, however, would not be easy.

The *Matildas* lagged behind other nations when it came to squad depth and game time according to Football Australia's 2020 "Women's Performance Gap Report". Just eight players had debuted between 2017 and 2020, and there was an over-reliance on a small core of *Matildas*, making the team vulnerable to injuries.

More matches against top European opposition were also needed if they were to debunk Australia's reputation of struggling against those types of teams. New government funding would allow for eight additional friendlies

ABOVE: The *Matildas* are three-time quarter-finalists – can they go further on home soil?

in the run-up to 2023; it was down to the new coach to build depth and experience.

The global pandemic meant it was April 2021 before Gustavsson got to meet his charges; his players had been apart for almost 13 months.

By the time they stepped out at the Olympics in July, they had lost to Germany, the Netherlands, Denmark and Japan, and had drawn with Sweden. They had coped with injuries and tested seven new players, but it had been a challenging programme and the pressure was on.

Buying into the manager's "never say die" culture and prepped after five weeks together in camp, the *Matildas* went on to surpass expectations in Japan. There were losses, but an epic seven-goal extra-time quarter-final thriller against Team GB saw Australia deliver a best-ever Olympic finish of fourth.

An experienced group carried them through, but young attacker Mary Fowler had scored and recent debutants, goalkeeper Teagan Micah and forward Kyra Cooney-Cross, picked up valuable minutes.

The nation got behind their team too, with 2.32 million tuning in at home to watch their heartbreaking 1-0 defeat by Sweden in the semi-final.

There would be no long run in the AFC Women's Asian Cup in January 2022, though, as Australia succumbed to a shock 1-0 quarter-final loss to Korea Republic. After hailing his players ahead of that tie for their aggression, high press and bravery, Gustavsson was left admiring their "family feeling" and camaraderie.

Mixed results followed with a win over New Zealand, then defeats to Spain and Canada. However, in late 2022, the *Matildas* finally

MARY FOWLER
BORN: 14 FEBRUARY 2003
POSITION: FORWARD

Hailing from a footballing family, this cool, speedy, two-footed attacker had yet to feature in a senior club game when she became the *Matildas*' fifth-youngest debutant aged 15. Joined W-League outfit Adelaide United in 2019 and scored on her debut. Still only 16 years old when she switched to French top-flight side Montpellier HSC, she would bag 10 goals in 40 appearances before moving to Manchester City in 2022. Scored the third goal against Team GB at the Tokyo Games and was named Australia's PFA Young Women's Footballer of the Year and a European Golden Girl nominee in 2022.

STEPH CATLEY
BORN: 26 JANUARY 1994
POSITION: DEFENDER

The *Matildas*' vice-captain is a popular yet humble leader and arguably one of the best left-backs in the world; versatile, with great vision and footballing nous. As a child, she talked her mum into letting her join her brother Dan's boys' club and has gone on to win a century of Australia caps. Started out with hometown club Melbourne Victory, going on to play for Portland Thorns, Orlando Pride and Reign FC in the USA. Joined Arsenal in the English Women's Super League in 2020 and after an injury-hit start has become a mainstay for the Gunners. Her partner Dean Bouzanis is also a professional footballer.

delivered – South Africa, Denmark and Sweden were all beaten, with 11 goals scored, two conceded.

Since facing Germany in April 2021, the *Matildas* had gained experience against most of the world's top ten sides, smashed attendance records and blooded 17 new players.

Sam Kerr had taken the crown as her nation's record scorer, male or female; new faces had emerged – Kerr and seven of her team mates had all become centurions.

They have all put in the hard yards – could this home FIFA Women's World Cup see them reap the rewards?

WOMEN'S WORLD CUP RECORD

1991	Did not qualify
1995	Group stage (4th)
1999	Group stage (3rd)
2003	Group stage (4th)
2007	Quarter-finalists
2011	Quarter-finalists
2015	Quarter-finalists
2019	Round of 16

< 45 >

REPUBLIC OF IRELAND

The Republic of Ireland will write a new chapter in their 50-year history when they walk out at this FIFA Women's World Cup. They pulled out all the stops to reach their maiden major tournament and will make the most of every minute in the global spotlight.

COACH
VERA PAUW

A triplet who honed her skills on the streets alongside her brothers, Pauw went on to win 85 official caps for the Netherlands and has broken new ground throughout her career. The first Dutch woman to play professionally in *Serie A*, she was the first to gain the UEFA Pro Licence and, as a coach, the first to lead the Netherlands to a major finals – taking her side to the 2009 UEFA Women's EURO semi-finals, where they lost in extra time to England. Having also overseen Scotland, Russia, South Africa, and US outfit Houston Dash, she joined the Republic of Ireland in 2019, and by 2022 had taken them to a FIFA/Coca-Cola Women's World Ranking high of 23.

A fire engine siren blared out across the runway to greet the Republic of Ireland players and staff off their plane at Dublin airport in October 2022. The *Girls in Green* had just gone toe-to-toe with Scotland in Glasgow in a winner-takes-all FIFA Women's World Cup play-off and they were returning home as history-makers.

Almost 33 years after the men had booked their first ticket to the finals, the women were set to follow in their footsteps – but it was a close-run contest in front of more than 10,000 fans at Hampden Park.

Republic of Ireland 'keeper Courtney Brosnan dug deep to deny Caroline Weir from the penalty spot; Scotland's Sophie Howard heroically cleared two goal-bound efforts off the line.

Ultimately, substitute Amber Barrett settled matters, keeping her head to coolly slot home on 72 minutes after deftly collecting Denise O'Sullivan's expertly delivered through-ball.

A lively bunch of travelling fans, friends and family were in raptures and, after seeing out their historic win, the players' pride at full time was there for all to see.

Less than two years earlier, Barrett and nine of the starting XI had seen their dreams of a 2022 UEFA Women's EURO play-off place finally extinguished by Germany.

That campaign had, though, seen a record-breaking crowd

ABOVE: Republic of Ireland are elated to qualify for their first major finals.

< 46 >

cheer them on to victory in Dublin against Ukraine, while the team's profile had grown with all matches live on TV.

After head coach Vera Pauw agreed to stay on for their impending FIFA Women's World Cup qualification campaign, even greater gains were to come.

In late August 2021, an equal pay deal was agreed for the women, with the men's squad and Football Association of Ireland covering the costs. That was swiftly followed by a landmark sponsorship deal just for the women's team.

It was a world away from 2017, when a group of national-team players had bravely stood up and called on the FAI to provide "basics" such as their own tracksuits, match fees, gym membership and access to a nutritionist. Yet if the new funding agreements meant more was expected of the team, they were ready to deliver.

With Pauw a firm believer in the value of friendlies against higher-ranked opponents, they had earlier faced, and narrowly lost to, Denmark, Belgium and Iceland. In their next outing, however, they stunned Australia 3-2.

By the time Ireland closed out their FIFA Women's World Cup qualifying campaign just over 12 months later, they had scored 27 goals and conceded just four. They had held world number two side Sweden to a draw in Gothenburg and beaten Finland in both Helsinki and at a sold-out Tallaght Stadium in Dublin.

"We've got identity in how we play, we've got a structure and style that we believe in and that we give 100 per cent with," captain Katie McCabe had said before their final campaign victory.

It was true: a blend of home-based players, US college footballers and professionals

KATIE MCCABE
BORN: 21 SEPTEMBER 1995
POSITION: MIDFIELDER

An outstanding left-footer who will put her body on the line for club and country and always offers a threat at set pieces. Won titles at home with Raheny United, on loan at Glasgow City and with Arsenal, where she was crowned player of the season for 2020-21. A semi-finalist with Ireland in the 2014 UEFA Women's U-19 Championship, she made her senior debut the following year. Handed the captaincy aged 21, she is an inspirational leader, never shirking responsibility. Dubbed the "assist queen", she also led the scoring charts for Ireland in qualifying. Her brother Gary is a former professional footballer.

DENISE O'SULLIVAN
BORN: 4 FEBRUARY 1994
POSITION: MIDFIELDER

A stylish and energetic playmaker who started out playing against boys in Cork. As a youth international she reached the UEFA Women's U-17 Championship final in 2010. Hit a brace on her first-team debut the following year. Ireland's senior women's player of 2015 and 2020, she was fast approaching a century of caps during FIFA Women's World Cup qualifying in 2022. A multiple title-winner with Glasgow City, she has proved her class in America's National Women's Soccer League. Twice named most valuable player for North Carolina Courage on their way to consecutive titles.

from top clubs overseas had embraced Pauw's game plans and performed when it mattered.

New faces like midfielders Lily Agg and Lucy Quinn had successfully bedded in among them, ever-present 'keeper Brosnan had come into her own, while a host of veterans had stepped up to lead the way.

They remembered those who had gone before them when they celebrated their FIFA Women's World Cup qualification achievement. Now it is time for the *Girls in Green* to blaze their own trail once again.

WOMEN'S WORLD CUP RECORD

A determined 1-0 play-off victory over Scotland in Glasgow saw the Republic of Ireland reach their maiden FIFA Women's World Cup. This was success at last in their seventh qualifying campaign for the global finals.

< 47 >

● NIGERIA

Nigeria are one of only seven nations to have featured in every edition of the FIFA Women's World Cup. Having reached the knockouts for the first time in two decades last time out, the *Super Falcons* will be determined to build again in 2023.

COACH
RANDY WALDRUM

The 66-year-old former Trinidad and Tobago boss was appointed to lead the *Super Falcons* in October 2020, combining the role with coaching the University of Pittsburgh's women's team. A former American Soccer League midfielder, the Texan is a respected figure on the US college soccer scene. Twice crowned national coach of the year, in his 15 seasons at the University of Notre Dame he led the women's side to two national titles and seven Big East Championships. Worked alongside some of the world's biggest names while at the helm of Houston Dash in the USA's National Women's Soccer League between 2014 and 2017 and has previously coached several of the USA's youth teams.

For so long the powerhouse of African football, the *Super Falcons* have endured mixed fortunes since their battling round-of-16 loss to then-world number two Germany at France 2019.

In the immediate aftermath, there was a pay dispute with the Nigeria Football Federation to settle. By October, head coach Thomas Dennerby had resigned and the dream of an Olympic Games berth had been crushed by Côte d'Ivoire on the away-goals rule.

They finally got back on the grass in February 2021, the ink on American coach Randy Waldrum's contract barely dry as he led them straight into tournament football at the four-team Turkish Women's Cup.

They won that title and would go on to draw with Portugal, but lose out to Jamaica and the USA in the USWNT's Summer Series. Seeing South Africa beat them to lift the home Aisha Buhari Cup was a bitter pill to swallow.

Crucially, they came through tricky Women's Africa Cup of Nations (WAFCON) qualifiers against historic rivals Ghana and Côte d'Ivoire to reach a competition they have dominated since their founding year in 1991.

Just as pleasing for Waldrum in his first year was the emergence of several new faces. American-born National Women's Soccer League players Michelle Alozie and

ABOVE: The *Super Falcons* have been proudly ever-present at the FIFA Women's World Cup.

Ifeoma Onumonu, and sisters Toni and Nicole Payne, had all impressed, as had African Games-winning captain Gift Monday and former England youth international and Women's Super League player Ashleigh Plumptre.

Several of those newcomers were part of a loss and draw friendly double-header with Olympic champions Canada. It was a solid test, but the WAFCON title defence that followed would offer an even greater challenge.

Captained by Onome Ebi, the first African player to feature at five FIFA Women's World Cups, the 11-time champions arrived in Morocco with over half the squad made up of continental championship debutants.

The entire group had to rally after losing both the opener to 2018 beaten finalists South Africa and talismanic striker Asisat Oshoala to a tournament-ending knee injury.

With noisy backing from dancing fans kitted out with drums and *vuvuzelas*, the *Super Falcons* bounced back with emphatic wins over Botswana and Burundi. Rasheedat Ajibade would give Nigeria supporters even more to cheer as she headed in the goal that beat Cameroon to deliver a coveted ticket to Australia & New Zealand 2023.

That would be as good as it got, though. Down to nine after two red cards, Nigeria almost edged the semi-final against hosts Morocco, but with the crowd of over 45,000 at fever pitch, they lost 5-4 in a penalty shoot-out.

A dispute over unpaid bonuses followed, before defeat to Zambia in the third place play-off saw the *Super Falcons* bow out without a medal for only the second time ever. It was not the ending Nigeria were used to

RASHEEDAT AJIBADE
BORN: 8 DECEMBER 1999
POSITION: FORWARD

The self-styled "girl with the blue hair" made the WAFCON Best XI in 2022 for her pace and eye for goal. An accounting graduate with diplomas in sport management and coaching psychology, she started her football career at FC Robo Queens. Gained top-table experience in four FIFA youth Women's World Cups and impressed as a teenage substitute against Germany at France 2019. Shone in Norway's *Toppserien* with Avaldsnes and continued that trajectory in Spain with Atlético Madrid. Her "Stand out with RASH" campaign aims to empower grassroots talent in her homeland.

CHIAMAKA NNADOZIE
BORN: 8 DECEMBER 2000
POSITION: GOALKEEPER

This former Rivers Angels shot-stopper has been Nigeria's number-one choice since France 2019 when, aged 18 years and 186 days, she became the youngest goalkeeper to play an entire FIFA Women's World Cup match without conceding. Went on to win 2019 African Games gold with the U-20s, saving three penalties in the final against Cameroon. A commanding six-footer, she has made her mark on the French top flight since joining Paris FC in January 2020. Nominated for the D1 best goalkeeper award in 2022, she won the Bruno Martini trophy for being the "revelation" of the division.

and they will arrive at the FIFA Women's World Cup without the continental crown in their locker, a situation they have never faced before.

Yet this is a nation with a proud history in the women's game and theirs is a team in transition. The future talent is there too, as Nigeria's FIFA U-20 Women's World Cup quarter-finalists showed with wins over France, Korea Republic and Canada last summer.

So with time and support, there is every chance that a blend of exciting newcomers and

established regulars can write a new story when they step out on this world stage.

WOMEN'S WORLD CUP RECORD

1991	Group stage (4th)
1995	Group stage (4th)
1999	Quarter-finalists
2003	Group stage (4th)
2007	Group stage (4th)
2011	Group stage (3rd)
2015	Group stage (4th)
2019	Round of 16

< 49 >

CANADA

It is two decades since Canada recorded their best finish at the FIFA Women's World Cup. Fourth back in 2003, the reigning Olympic champions have targeted first place at Australia & New Zealand 2023 and will arrive having done all they can to prepare.

COACH
BEV PRIESTMAN

Born in England's North East, the 37-year-old is a driven, approachable coach who thrives on pressure. Worked in youth football with New Zealand and Canada. Led Canada's U-17s to the FIFA Women's World Cup quarter-final in 2014. Was head coach of the U-20s while also gaining vital experience with Canada's seniors as John Herdman's assistant in the FIFA Women's World Cup 2015 and bronze-medal winning Rio Olympics. Appointed Phil Neville's No. 2 with England in 2018, she helped take the team to fourth at France 2019. Got her chance as a No. 1 with a return to Canada in November 2020 and less than a year later secured Olympic gold. Named IFFHS Women's World Best National Coach in 2021.

When Canada won gold at the Tokyo Games in 2021, they did not view it as job done, but as the start of a journey they hoped would lead to this year's FIFA Women's World Cup and a lasting legacy.

The *Canucks* had won bronze at the previous two Olympics but, in less than a year under new coach Bev Priestman, they had addressed any defensive frailties and found their self-belief.

Yes, they scraped through the group stage, but they went on to overcome Brazil and four-time gold medallists the USA before winning a gripping penalty shoot-out final with Sweden, their conquerors at France 2019.

A bar had been set and now they were determined to raise it with a place at Australia & New Zealand 2023 via the Concacaf W Championship.

With a bye to the eight-nation finals and a year to prepare, Canada embarked on a string of friendlies aimed at exposing the players to the kind of quality and styles they might face should they reach the global showpiece.

At the Arnold Clark Cup in February 2022, three of Europe's top ten sides posed questions of a Canada outfit that still needed to find its ruthless edge.

After drawing 1-1 with hosts England, beating Germany 1-0 but losing by the odd goal to Spain, Priestman took the positives,

ABOVE: The Olympic champions Canada are hungry for further success.

< 50 >

which included the way her out-of-season players had adapted to tournament-level intensity.

With a subsequent 2-0 win then a 2-2 draw with African giants Nigeria, and a goalless stalemate with Korea Republic, Canada were as ready as they could be.

Aiming to stop them in the continental championship were three teams looking to avenge losses in 2018, when a squad that included five teenagers led Canada to a runners-up spot.

This Concacaf squad of 23 included four new faces and 18 gold medallists. There were four 30-somethings in there and three of them, Sophie Schmidt, Desiree Scott and Christine Sinclair, had played their part when Canada had last been crowned Concacaf champions, back in 2010.

Scott and Sinclair would feature in their opening match, the world's leading scorer "Sinc" notching up her 190th international goal with a header in the first half against Trinidad & Tobago. Needing to put the game to bed, Priestman told her team to "take the handbrake off" at half-time and they went on to unleash an avalanche, five late goals sealing a 6-0 win.

Just as four years earlier, Canada's FIFA Women's World Cup ambitions now required a result against Panama. There was no seven-goal rout this time, one goal settling it, courtesy of winning Olympic penalty spot-kick heroine Julia Grosso.

Canada's ticket to the global finals had been stamped but, after seeing off Costa Rica 2-0, then Jamaica 3-0 in the semi-final, they were beaten to the Concacaf title by the USA yet again through an Alex Morgan penalty.

As pick-me-ups go, two subsequent friendly wins Down

JESSIE FLEMING
BORN: 11 MARCH 1998
POSITION: MIDFIELDER

A hard-working playmaker with outstanding technique, she debuted for Canada at 15 and was a centurion at 24. A veteran of two Olympics and two FIFA Women's World Cups, she scored the spot kick that beat rivals the USA in the Tokyo Olympics and one in the final too. Canada's Soccer Player of the Year in 2021 and again in 2022, her leadership skills have been likened to Christine Sinclair's. Ranked ninth in the 2021 *Ballon d'Or féminin*, she is a fans' favourite at Chelsea, where she has won a string of major titles. She also loves to ride her bike around England's capital city, London.

JANINE BECKIE
BORN: 20 AUGUST 1994
POSITION: FORWARD

A world-class player, whose crossing ability and one-touch play make her a key part of any team. An Olympic bronze and gold medallist, she scored within 20 seconds at Rio 2016 – the competition's fastest-ever goal. Began her professional career with Houston Dash then Sky Blue FC in the National Women's Soccer League. Scored key goals in four seasons with English WSL side Manchester City, including the deciding penalty in the 2019 League Cup final shoot-out and another in the victorious FA Cup final of 2020. Moved to Portland Thorns last April, winning the NWSL Championship in her first season.

Under against Australia and in Spain over Argentina and Morocco were quite the tonic.

With players missing through injury, Canada had proved they had strength in depth. It was clear that talismanic players like Sinclair could still contribute, young talent such as speedy attacker Clarissa Larisey and FIFA U-20 Women's World Cup skipper Jade Rose are ones for the future, and regulars like Adriana Leon can be irrepressible in attack.

Their journey to Australia & New Zealand 2023 had begun; the

only destination Canada have in mind now is Sydney to lift the coveted trophy.

WOMEN'S WORLD CUP RECORD

1991	Did not qualify
1995	Group stage (3rd)
1999	Group stage (3rd)
2003	Fourth place
2007	Group stage (3rd)
2011	Group stage (4th)
2015	Quarter-finalists
2019	Round of 16

< 51 >

SPAIN

La Roja have yet to progress further than the last 16 in two attempts at a FIFA Women's World Cup. However, their stock has risen considerably since that first appearance eight years ago, and their style and quality attract much admiration.

COACH
JORGE VILDA

After his own promising playing career was prematurely cut short by a knee condition, he diverted his energy and ambition into coaching, first taking charge of the women's U-17s in 2009, aged 27. After winning two European gold medals, three silvers and a bronze with the U-17s and U-19s, he also claimed silver at the FIFA U-17 Women's World Cup in 2014 before taking the reins of the senior side in 2015. An advocate of attractive football, he has been sporting director of the Spanish women's teams since June 2018, responsible for the "playing philosophy and methodology" of the programme. He also tutors on tactics at the Spanish FA's National Coaching Academy, instructing many ex-professionals like Xabi Alonso, Xavi and his own assistant, Laura del Río.

For a nation that has long been in thrall to the beautiful game, Spain's women's team were late to arrive on the global stage. Their first appearance in a world finals was at Canada 2015 and, after a semi-final finish at the European Championship in 1997, they did not return to the continental top table until 2013.

La Roja's brand of possession football is a treat for spectators but historically has failed to translate into goals or results in key contests and their tournament record is underwhelming.

In 2015, they drew 1-1 with fellow debutants Costa Rica, but lost to Brazil and Korea Republic and finished bottom of their group.

It was a disappointment that led to the departure of long-time coach Ignacio Quereda, after 27 years at the helm, and the installation of then 34-year-old Jorge Vilda.

Four years later in France, armed with growing belief, they fared better. They beat South Africa 3-1 – their first-ever victory in the competition – lost 1-0 to Germany and drew 0-0 with China PR. This teed up a round-of-16 tie against the USA, but two Megan Rapinoe penalties saw the eventual champions prevail 2-1.

Learning that they could compete against the elite elevated confidence and expectations, as did the emergence of Barcelona – UEFA Women's Champions League winners in 2021 and runners-up in

ABOVE: Spain qualified with eight wins, 53 goals scored and zero conceded.

2019 and 2022 – as an elite force in European competition.

The Spanish top flight turned fully professional for the 2021-22 season and world-record crowds of 91,553 and then 91,648 roared on the treble winners at the Camp Nou in March and April 2022.

Spanish women's football was on a high and the squad headed to EURO 2022 feeling their time had come. Unfortunately, injuries to striker Jennifer Hermoso and the reigning Best FIFA Women's Player Alexia Putellas would severely dent their chances.

In a tough group, they dismissed Finland 4-1, lost 2-0 to Germany and beat Denmark 1-0 courtesy of a 90th-minute header by Marta Cardona. In the end, their ambitions were quashed by eventual champions England, the hosts edging them 2-1 during extra time in a thrilling quarter-final.

Meanwhile, eight straight wins, 53 goals for and zero conceded meant qualifying for Australia & New Zealand 2023 was a breeze.

Then, in September 2022, a dissatisfied collective of 15 prominent La Roja regulars – including a number of Barça players – publicly declared themselves unavailable for selection unless there was a change in group management or methods.

The Spanish FA denounced the move and backed Vilda, declaring the intention to build a "new" national team with players who were "committed". Only 11 players from the previous squad were reselected, with a sizeable Real Madrid contingent and personnel drawn from the U-23s and U-20s.

They hit the ground running in October against two teams ranked in the world's top three, drawing 1-1 with Sweden and then pulling off a historic

ATHENEA DEL CASTILLO
BORN: 24 OCTOBER 2000
POSITION: FORWARD

An exciting wide player who can operate on either flank. She has electric pace, a fierce strike and mesmerising dribbling skills which delight crowds and torment opposing defenders. Signed for Real Madrid in the summer of 2021 and has said: "I've been a *Madridista* since I was little … if I had to, I'd pay to play for Real Madrid." An U-19 European champion in 2018, she made her national-team debut the day before her 20th birthday. Was drafted into the squad for the 2022 Arnold Clark Cup as a late replacement and went on to be named player of the tournament.

ESTHER GONZÁLEZ
BORN: 8 DECEMBER 1992
POSITION: FORWARD

A busy, talkative, poacher of a centre-forward who excels at link-up play. Was top scorer and the only girl in the team in her native Granada. Aged 14 she had to switch to a women's team, requiring a 250km commute, to continue playing. Her clubs include CD Algaidas, Levante UD, Málaga, Sporting Huelva and Atlético Madrid, with whom she won the cup and three league titles. Signed for Real Madrid in 2021, scored nine in six games in World Cup qualifying and recovered from an ankle injury to make the EURO squad. Studying physiotherapy and is one of the three new captains of La Roja.

first-ever win against world champions the USA, 2-0. La Roja subsequently leapt to a new high of sixth in the world ranking.

Other nations could have struggled in this scenario but Spain's player development and achievements on a global and continental youth level are remarkable. They were back-to-back champions of the FIFA U-17 Women's World Cup in 2018 and 2022 and winners of the FIFA U-20 Women's World Cup in 2022 too.

Does this newer generation have the nous to get results under pressure against the best? Will we

see a mixed squad with reconciled La Roja stars? Either way, Spain will be contenders.

WOMEN'S WORLD CUP RECORD

1991	Did not qualify
1995	Did not qualify
1999	Did not qualify
2003	Did not qualify
2007	Did not qualify
2011	Did not qualify
2015	Group stage (4th)
2019	Round of 16

< 53 >

COSTA RICA

Costa Rica departed their maiden FIFA Women's World Cup in 2015 having carved out a higher profile worldwide with draws against Spain and Korea Republic in the group stage. Eight years on, *Las Ticas* are gearing up to make an impression once more.

COACH
AMELIA VALVERDE

Developed a love of football from an early age, going on to play in defence for first-division outfit Flores, becoming their head coach when she was just 22. Joined Costa Rica as physical trainer in 2011 before taking roles with the U-17s and U-20s. Switched from assistant to head coach in 2015, mere months before their FIFA Women's World Cup debut, where her team won praise for their discipline, organisation and determination. Named Concacaf Female Coach of the Year in 2016, this focused and analytical 36-year-old has gone on to secure success in a host of regional competitions as well as another FIFA Women's World Cup spot, all the while championing improvements for the entire national set-up.

Costa Rica were one of eight nations with their eyes on the prize of an automatic FIFA Women's World Cup ticket when they arrived in Mexico for the Concacaf W Championship last summer.

Four places were up for grabs via the regional tournament and Costa Rica were eager to repeat their feat of 2014, when a best-ever finish of second delivered a maiden berth at the global finals.

For head coach Amelia Valverde and 14 of her 2022 squad, the memory of that debut on the world stage still burned brightly. Yes, they exited Canada 2015 early, but they did so with their worldwide reputation enhanced.

A unified group followed up with 2017 Central American Games gold, 2018 Central American and Caribbean Games silver and 2019 Pan American Games bronze.

Yet the dream of consecutive world finals appearances failed to materialise, dashed in 2018 by losses in the continental championship to Jamaica and Canada.

So after bouncing back with just two defeats in eight friendlies after a year-long competitive absence caused by the global pandemic, they were raring to try again in 2022.

Reaching the championship that would decide their FIFA Women's World Cup fate was relatively straightforward, staying

ABOVE: Returning for their second finals appearance, Costa Rica continue to impress.

< 54 >

unbeaten in a campaign that finished with a 5-0 win over Guatemala in front of 6,500 fans in San José.

Carrying that form to Mexico, they got off to a dream start, with Raquel Rodríguez, María Paula Salas and captain Katherine Alvarado scoring in an emphatic win over Panama.

In their second outing, a brace from Cristín Granados, a deflection and a spectacular Alvarado goal from distance brushed aside ten-player Trinidad & Tobago.

At full time, the team tossed trailblazing No. 10 Shirley Cruz into the air to celebrate her 100th cap at the age of 36. That night, a group of veterans and exciting new talent had even more to toast.

They had to wait to be sure but, when group rivals Canada beat Panama in the evening match, Costa Rica's ticket to Australia & New Zealand 2023 was assured.

"*Lo hicimos!* We did it!" Cruz declared on Twitter and the talk when they met officials at the Presidential House the following month was of the "happiness" they had brought their football-obsessed country.

Finishing fourth after losses to perennial bogey teams Canada and the USA, as well as Jamaica in the battle for third and an Olympic play-off spot, showed there was work to be done.

Costa Rica would not stand still, though. A plan to afford a mostly home-based amateur squad national team time was swiftly agreed with the Costa Rican FA (FCRF), the league and clubs.

Top-level friendlies and even improvements such as the FCRF installing a new grass pitch solely for the women to train on will have aided preparations too.

As for a squad that includes players with experience gained at

RAQUEL RODRÍGUEZ
BORN: 28 OCTOBER 1993
POSITION: MIDFIELDER/ FORWARD

"Rocky" is a skilful player who thrives under pressure. Can take a deft touch and find a clever pass in the tightest of spaces and is a natural goalscorer too. Wrote her name into Costa Rican history as the scorer of their first-ever youth and senior FIFA Women's World Cup goals. Won multiple awards at American college Penn State, including the prestigious MAC Hermann Trophy as the top college soccer player before joining Sky Blue then, in 2020, Portland Thorns in the National Women's Soccer League. Played her part in the Thorns' NWSL Championship-winning run in 2022.

PRISCILA CHINCHILLA
BORN: 11 JULY 2001
POSITION: MIDFIELDER

Honed her skills at a boys' academy and is a simply thrilling prospect who can tear opponents apart with her trickery. A league winner in Costa Rica with Liga Deportiva Alajuelense, where she top-scored for two years in a row, she joined Scottish champions Glasgow City aged 19 and soon made her mark, winning the league title in her first season. The following year, with 22 goals in 35 appearances, she won both the first-ever PFA Scotland and SWPL 1 player of the year awards. Also made the PFA Scotland Team of the Year. Now fluent in English, she is one of Scotland's most popular players.

world youth championships and in top leagues in Mexico, the USA and Europe, once qualification was assured, Valverde insisted the door was open.

Stars of last year's hugely popular home FIFA U-20 Women's World Cup, such as captain Alexandra Pinell and defender Abigail Sancho, are already knocking.

From youth sides to seniors, Costa Rica has taken great strides since a group of trailblazers made their official tournament debut in 1991. Having already contributed so much,

this generation will look to lay yet more paths for progress at Australia & New Zealand 2023.

WOMEN'S WORLD CUP RECORD

1991	Did not qualify
1995	Did not enter
1999	Did not qualify
2003	Did not qualify
2007	Did not qualify
2011	Did not qualify
2015	Group stage (3rd)
2019	Did not qualify

< 55 >

ZAMBIA

Zambia are fast establishing themselves as a force to be reckoned with in the women's game in Africa. The *Copper Queens* will look to enhance that reputation even further when they take their first steps at the FIFA Women's World Cup.

COACH
BRUCE MWAPE

Former boss of men's side Nchanga Rangers in the Zambian Super League, the veteran coach was appointed *Copper Queens* manager in 2018. Has gone on to lead Zambia to a series of historic firsts, from maiden berths at the Olympics and FIFA Women's World Cup, to winning WAFCON bronze and the COSAFA title. In 2022, he took Zambia to a new high of 80th in the FIFA/Coca-Cola Women's World Ranking. Claimed a personal accolade in 2021 when he was named the best national coach in Africa in the IFFHS Women's Continental Awards. Hails from Chingola in the Copperbelt region and was given a hero's welcome on his return from their WAFCON success, rewarded with a special plot of land from the local council.

Few fans will ever forget Zambia's last outing on the global stage. It came at the Tokyo Olympics in 2021, when the *Copper Queens* lit up the tournament with their never-say-die approach and cheery "penguin dance" goal celebration.

Their attacking brand of football won them fans too, with the debutants refusing to give up in a humbling 10-3 opening defeat to the Netherlands before drawing with China PR in an eight-goal thriller.

Bowing out to Brazil by a single goal, despite battling with 10 players for 80 minutes following an early red card, the lowest-ranked team in the 12-nation tournament proved they were not there just to make up the numbers.

At the COSAFA Women's Championship for southern African nations soon after, Bruce Mwape's players had to settle for bronze for the fourth time, having won silver in 2019.

But a resilient group broke new ground again in 2022 with a remarkable run in the Women's Africa Cup of Nations that yielded both a medal and a maiden FIFA Women's World Cup berth.

Green Buffaloes' Zambian championship-winning defenders Martha Tembo and Agness Musase, and ZISD Queens' midfielder Evarine Susan Katongo, would start every game, with

ABOVE: Entertainers Zambia will fear no one at their maiden FIFA Women's World Cup.

< 56 >

fellow home-based players Avell Chitundu and Lushomo Mweemba also key. And with talismanic skipper Barbra Banda ruled out after failing gender eligibility tests, her fellow FIFA U-17 Women's World Cup 2014 veterans Margaret Belemu, Grace Chanda and Ireen Lungu, goalkeeper Hazel Nali and Mary Wilombe stepped up to the plate.

Defensively resilient, Zambia battled to a goalless draw with four-time finalists Cameroon, before bettering their previous WAFCON finals tally with victories over Tunisia and debutants Togo.

Senegal fell next, seen off in a quarter-final penalty shoot-out – 'keeper Nali the heroine after saving and scoring to send Zambia to a historic first berth at the FIFA Women's World Cup.

With just the semi-final against South Africa standing between them and the final, the team could sense the impact they were having at home as goodwill messages flooded in. "You can feel the excitement that is spreading throughout the country," said Mwape. "Thanks to social networks, our team remains connected to our people."

Their dream final was not to be, though, Zambia losing to South Africa through a controversial injury-time penalty that was awarded after a VAR review.

Even so, they rallied to edge the third-place play-off against reigning WAFCON champions Nigeria, 1-0, and claim a first-ever bronze medal.

Women's football has come a long way since being recognised by the FA of Zambia in 1983 and the *Copper Queens* were rightly feted on their return home. A buoyant squad was driven on a "thank you" parade and several players were rewarded with promotions in the Zambian army.

BARBRA BANDA
BORN: 20 MARCH 2000
POSITION: FORWARD

A genuine star turn and prolific striker, the team captain was just 13 when she debuted in the FIFA U-17 Women's World Cup. By 21, she was the first woman to hit consecutive hat-tricks at a single Olympic Games. Became the first Zambian woman to play in Spain's top flight in 2018 when she joined EDF Logroño. Moved on to Chinese Women's Super League outfit Shanghai Shengli, bagging twice as many goals as the next highest scorer in her debut season. Led Zambia to the 2022 COSAFA title, crowned as player of the tournament and golden boot winner with ten goals. She is also a talented boxer.

GRACE CHANDA
BORN: 11 JUNE 1997
POSITION: FORWARD

Captained Zambia to bronze at last summer's WAFCON. Named in the tournament's Best XI – and nominated for African Player of the Year midway through – the colourfully coiffured attacker thrilled with her pace, goals and selfless play. At 16, she bagged Zambia's only goal in the FIFA U-17 Women's World Cup in 2014. Crowned best player and top scorer at Zambia's inaugural Women in Football Awards in 2021 after netting 35 goals in 26 games for Red Arrows. Enjoyed a successful spell with Kazakhstan outfit BIIK-Kazygurt, scoring a hat-trick on her debut in UEFA Women's Champions League qualifying.

Seven weeks later, Zambia gained revenge over South Africa to win a first COSAFA crown. It was another outstanding campaign, with player of the tournament Barbra Banda and golden glove winner Catherine Musonda in sensational form.

The depth of talent was clear too, as teenagers Eneless Phiri, Judith Soko, Esther Siamfuko and Maweta Glory Chilenga all seized their chances.

How brightly the *Copper Queens* can shine at this global showpiece remains to be seen, but we can be sure that a talented group will give their all to rise to the occasion.

WOMEN'S WORLD CUP RECORD

Debutants Zambia are the seventh African team ever to reach the FIFA Women's World Cup. They booked their spot via a top-four finish at the Women's Africa Cup of Nations, beating Senegal on penalties in the quarter-final.

< 57 >

JAPAN

Former winners in 2011 and finalists in 2015, the *Nadeshiko* still boast an abundance of emerging talent and technical performers and play a familiar, crowd-pleasing style of passing football, but can the current team match the remarkable standards set by their predecessors?

COACH
FUTOSHI IKEDA

Played as a defender for Urawa Red Diamonds in Japan's top flight between 1993 and 1996 before turning to coaching and assisting the same club through a number of youth age groups. Began working with *Young Nadeshiko* squads in 2017 after four years coaching at J1 League side Avispa Fukuoka. Steered his stylish side to success at the FIFA U-20 Women's World Cup in 2018, a feat which meant Japan became the first country in the world to win all three categories of the FIFA Women's World Cup. Stepped up to manage the senior women's national team in October 2021, 40 years after their formation. Oversaw another U-20s silver medal in Costa Rica in 2022.

The fairytale-like quality of Japan's triumph in Frankfurt in 2011, when they battled back to beat the USA on penalties, is one of the tournament's most enduring and magical memories.

Under then-coach Norio Sasaki, Japan also went on to win silver at London 2012 and faced the USA again in the FIFA Women's World Cup final in Canada, but were stunned by Carli Lloyd's hat-trick in the opening 16 minutes and lost 5-2.

Although there were AFC title successes in 2014 and 2018 and *Young Nadeshiko* (U-20s) teams continue to impress on the global stage, Japan failed to qualify for the Rio Olympics in 2016 and had poor showings at the FIFA Women's World Cup 2019 and the Tokyo Games in 2021.

These setbacks led to a degree of self-reflection and Asako Takakura stepped down as manager when her contract expired a month after their home Olympics. She had overseen a five-year period of rebuilding, waving goodbye to the "golden generation" and phasing in fresh talent.

With this next chapter in mind, the Japan FA turned to 2018 FIFA U-20 Women's World Cup-winning coach Futoshi Ikeda and a three-year project to help reclaim their position as the best in the world.

Another forward-thinking initiative was the introduction of the fully professional Japan Women's

ABOVE: Champions in 2011 and runners-up four years later, Japan's standards are high.

< 58 >

Empowerment Professional Football League (WE LEAGUE), a new elite division above the previous top-tier Nadeshiko League.

Its inaugural season ran in 2021-22 and, although spectator levels were lower than hoped, the competition's intentions to help grow the game are clear and standards should continue to improve year-on-year.

Goalkeeper Ayaka Yamashita, of title winners INAC Kobe Leonessa, was the league's first MVP, and established forward Yuika Sugasawa, with 14 goals, was top scorer. Also included in the end-of-season Best XI were defenders Risa Shimizu and Moeka Minami, both of whom subsequently made moves to Europe, signing for West Ham United and AS Roma, respectively.

They joined a number of other *Nadeshiko* players, testing themselves and developing in different competitions and cultures. Jun Endo, Hina Sugita and Fuka Nagano competed in the NWSL in the USA in 2022, while Yui Hasegawa joined Manchester City and Saori Takarada turned out for Linköpings FC. Among the overseas contingent, Saki Kumagai and Mana Iwabuchi have the highest profiles, both veterans of the 2011 victory.

Defensive lynchpin and skipper Kumagai lamented after the team's 3-1 quarter-final Olympic exit to a strong Sweden outfit in 2021: "We may be skilful, but it's not enough to win against the top teams."

This concise evaluation could also describe their story at the 2022 AFC Women's Asian Cup. It applied to the 1-1 group-stage draw with Korea Republic and the semi-final defeat on spot kicks when they should have put the game out of reach before China PR fought back to draw 2-2. In both matches they missed chances and conceded late levellers despite dominating.

ONES TO WATCH

RISA SHIMIZU
BORN: 15 JUNE 1996
POSITION: DEFENDER

Attacking and spirited right-back whose rousing overlapping runs add an exciting dimension to the team's attacking play. A *Nadeshiko* mainstay since her debut in February 2018, Shimizu is a former forward who was inspired to take up football by her older sister. Made over 200 appearances for Nippon TV Beleza, winning the league title five times in a row and the AFC Women's Club Championship in 2019. Named in the Nadeshiko League team of the season four years running, then first-ever WE League Best Eleven and included in AFC Women's Asian Cup 2022 Players to Watch too.

RIKO UEKI
BORN: 30 JULY 1999
POSITION: FORWARD

Nippon TV Beleza's highly promising striker. A runner-up at the FIFA U-17 Women's World Cup 2016 and a winner in 2018 at the U-20 edition in France. Sadly missed out on the senior tournament a year later due to injury but now really flourishing under the Ikeda regime. With only six prior caps, Ueki emerged as Japan's top scorer (five) at the 2022 Women's Asian Cup and featured in every game. Achieved a career goal by starting alongside her role model Mana Iwabuchi in the semi-final in India. Graduated in Sports Science from Waseda University in spring 2022 and is a massive fan of manga.

Opponents and spectators know that *Nadeshiko* teams will play a possession-based game with quick passing, overlapping full-backs and fluid, rotational movement between their midfielders and forwards. It is spellbinding and can overwhelm opposition when everything comes together.

"The *Nadeshiko Japan* became the world champions in 2011, so our goal is to build a team that can reclaim that title," announced Ikeda upon his appointment.

It is a bold aim but, as they have proved in the past, not an impossible one.

WOMEN'S WORLD CUP RECORD

1991	Group stage (4th)
1995	Quarter-finalists
1999	Group stage (4th)
2003	Group stage (3rd)
2007	Group stage (3rd)
2011	Winners
2015	Runners-up
2019	Round of 16

< 59 >

✚ ENGLAND

The newly crowned European champions romped through a record-breaking FIFA Women's World Cup qualifying campaign and are riding high on surging public support and interest. Semi-finalists in the last two editions, they will look to go all the way this time.

COACH
SARINA WIEGMAN

Kicking about with her brother escalated into an international call-up aged 16, a season at University of North Carolina and becoming the first Dutch footballer to reach 100 caps. Taught PE while still a player before retiring in 2003. Managed former club Ter Leede, then ADO Den Haag, spent a season assisting at men's club Sparta Rotterdam and twice stepped in as interim coach with the *Oranje Leeuwinnen*, firstly in 2015. Appointed permanently in January 2017, winning a home EURO six months later and silver at France 2019. Took over England in September 2021 and won their home EURO ten months later. The Best FIFA Women's Coach 2017 and 2020 and UEFA Women's Coach of the Year 2021/22.

A unified England realised their title-winning dreams in the summer of 2022 as their sensational run in the UEFA Women's EURO came to a triumphant conclusion.

Sarina Wiegman's side had seen off some of the biggest names on the continent on their way to a showpiece home final and, roared on by a competition record 87,192 fans at Wembley Stadium, they would overcome Germany too.

With an unchanged side and match-winning rookie substitutes, England's 8-0 group-stage thrashing of Norway, nail-biting extra-time quarter-final win over Spain and 4-0 rout of Sweden in the semi-final had already grabbed the nation's interest.

Their euphoric 2-1 extra-time final triumph took the team to another level entirely, England women's first-ever major trophy win lauded with wall-to-wall coverage, plus millions of interactions on social media.

England's players were the names on everyone's lips by the time they walked out to meet 7,000 well-wishers in front of a live television audience at a victory celebration at London's iconic Trafalgar Square the next day.

Wiegman's group could not and would not dwell, though, and by September they had secured a FIFA Women's World Cup spot, their ten clean-sheet wins and 80 goals the best record in UEFA women's qualifying history.

ABOVE: Current European champions England broke records for goalscoring in qualifying.

< 60 >

Remarkably, the architects of their success, Wiegman and her assistant Arjan Veurink, had only been part of the *Lionesses*' set-up for a year. England had reached the last four at EURO 2017 and France 2019, but they had gone through two head coaches and an interim boss since that time too.

With a national-team programme and a raft of staff supported financially by the English FA, increased broadcast deals, sponsorship and a full-time professional top flight, the expectation now was for stability and trophies.

Having sensationally led the unfancied Dutch to European gold and FIFA Women's World Cup silver, Wiegman was seen as the final piece in England's jigsaw and the former Netherlands captain was certainly a good fit.

In February, even as she tinkered with positions and line-ups, the *Lionesses* won the Arnold Clark Cup home invitational ahead of top-ten ranked sides Canada, Germany and Spain.

With the coach's focus on possession-based, dynamic, attacking football, they went on to rack up 68 FIFA Women's World Cup qualifying goals without conceding in Wiegman's first seven months in charge. Part of that included a 20-0 battering of Latvia, England's highest-ever victory. As their home EURO dawned, a winning momentum and mindset were already in motion.

Explaining the role she expected every one of her group to play at the tournament before a ball was even kicked, Wiegman kept the same starting XI for every match, throwing on game-changing substitutes Ella Toone, Alessia Russo and Chloe Kelly to great effect.

The star turn would prove to

LAUREN HEMP
BORN: 7 AUGUST 2000
POSITION: FORWARD

Super-speedy left-winger with a stellar future. Aged just 16 when she made her bow in the English top flight with Bristol City. In 2017, was crowned England Women's Young Player and, in 2018, won the first of an unprecedented four PFA Women's Young Player of the Year awards. Signed professional terms with Manchester City in 2018, bursting off the bench at Wembley to score on her Women's FA Cup final debut later that season. Won World Cup bronze with the U-20s in 2018 and excelled for Team GB in 2021. Scored her first four goals for England in a record 20-0 win over Latvia in 2021.

KEIRA WALSH
BORN: 8 APRIL 1997
POSITION: MIDFIELDER

Holding midfielder with fantastic poise, football intelligence and vision who studied and styled her game on midfield greats of the Spanish men's team. Joined her beloved Manchester City from Blackburn Rovers aged 17 and made her first start swiftly after in the 2014 League Cup final, going on to win every domestic honour and amassing more than 200 appearances for the club. Became a pivotal figure for England, and Team GB, following her senior debut in November 2017. Player of the Match in the UEFA Women's EURO 2022 final, Barcelona paid a reported world record fee of £400,000 to sign her a month later.

be forward Beth Mead with her Midas touch in front of goal, while Arsenal team-mate Leah Williamson wore the armband with a confidence that belied her 25 years.

Veterans of major tournaments past, Jill Scott and Ellen White, would also prove their worth in their last hurrah as England players on the way to a groundbreaking title win.

Competition for places is fierce and even in their "no blame" culture there is no room for sentimentality as the *Lionesses* look to Australia & New Zealand

2023. Sustained success is the aim, and so is the biggest prize of them all.

WOMEN'S WORLD CUP RECORD

1991	Did not qualify
1995	Quarter-finalists
1999	Did not qualify
2003	Did not qualify
2007	Quarter-finalists
2011	Quarter-finalists
2015	Third place
2019	Fourth place

< 61 >

CHILE

Such are the strides that have been made by *La Roja* in recent years, including intrepid displays in the last two global tournaments, anything but success in the inter–confederation play–offs could be considered a serious setback.

Anchored by inspirational skipper and world-class goalkeeper Christiane Endler, Chile showed their mettle at their maiden FIFA Women's World Cup in 2019. Following gutsy 2-0 and 3-0 defeats to Sweden and the USA – who went on to win bronze and gold, respectively – they earned a heartening 2-0 win over Thailand.

The quest to establish themselves firmly on the world stage gained further traction

two years later at the Tokyo Olympics, an opportunity secured via a two-legged intercontinental play-off against Cameroon. Again they proved tough opponents, only falling 2-0 to Team GB and by single goals to eventual winners Canada and hosts Japan.

Those performances at major tournaments were a remarkable achievement considering the neglect shown by the Chilean FA to the women's national team programme and lack of fixtures for the side between 2014 and 2017.

Given such impressive progress, perhaps more was expected at last year's *Copa América Femenina*, as the 2018 hosts and runners-up arrived in Colombia with

another FIFA Women's World Cup qualification firmly in their sights.

Caught off guard twice early on in their opener against an improving Paraguay, *La Roja* could not fully recover and were beaten 3-2. Despite rebounding with victories over Ecuador and Bolivia, a subsequent 4-0 loss to Colombia consigned them to a pressure tie against Venezuela for fifth place.

Although pegged back to 1-1 in stoppage time, Chile could rely on stalwarts like Francisca Lara and Karen Araya to hold their nerve in the shoot-out. They triumphed 4-2, thus securing a valued last chance to qualify for Australia & New Zealand 2023 through the inter-confederation play-offs.

COACH: JOSÉ LETELIER

ONES TO WATCH:
CHRISTIANE ENDLER
BORN: 23 JULY 1991
POSITION: GOALKEEPER

KAREN ARAYA
BORN: 16 OCTOBER 1990
POSITION: MIDFIELDER

ABOVE: Chilean players pose for a team shot before their 2022 *Copa América Femenina* match against Bolivia.
LEFT: José Letelier, head coach of Chile.

< 62 >

SENEGAL

Senegal gave the profile of women's football in their home nation a genuine boost when they sealed a FIFA Women's World Cup play-off spot.

COACH: MAME MOUSSA CISSÉ

ONES TO WATCH:
SAFIETOU SAGNA
BORN: 11 APRIL 1994
POSITION: MIDFIELDER

NGUENAR NDIAYE
BORN: 10 JANUARY 1995
POSITION: FORWARD

In 2022, Senegal returned to their continental championship, the Women's Africa Cup of Nations, after a decade-long absence.

They more than made up for lost time, enjoying group-stage wins over Uganda and Burkina Faso to record their first-ever goals and victories in the competition.

Their dream of an automatic ticket to Australia & New Zealand 2023 was dashed by Zambia in the worst of ways: a penalty shoot-out in the quarter-finals.

LEFT: Senegal were in action at the 2022 Women's Africa Cup of Nations after a ten-year hiatus.

The *Teranga Lionesses* rallied, however, beating Tunisia by the same 4-2 scoreline in another epic spot-kick battle to progress to February's inter-confederation play-offs.

Defensively strong with a stylish midfield and an exciting forward line, these West African players helped shine a positive light on the women's game in Senegal.

And with U-17 and U-20 teams coming through in the past ten years and senior players honing their talents in Europe, there is much more to come from these pioneers.

HAITI

Haiti's U-20s tasted life on the global stage in 2018, and now their ever-improving senior players are ready to make the next step forward.

COACH: NICOLAS DELÉPINE

ONES TO WATCH:
MELCHIE DUMORNAY
BORN: 17 AUGUST 2003
POSITION: MIDFIELDER

NÉRILIA MONDÉSIR
BORN: 17 JANUARY 1999
POSITION: FORWARD

It is five years since Haiti's U-20s became the first in their country to reach a FIFA Women's World Cup at any age level and, despite three losses, they were no pushovers in France.

A handful of those players, including goalscoring captain Nérilia Mondésir, are among those now aiming to add senior honours to that achievement.

They have already shown their ability with a perfect qualification for their sixth

LEFT: The *Grenadières*' line up ahead of an international friendly against Portugal in November 2022.

Concacaf W Championship that included a 21-0 win over British Virgin Islands among their four victories.

At last summer's finals, they missed chances to score in losses to the USA and Jamaica, but a 3-0 victory over Mexico proved crucial to their FIFA Women's World Cup hopes.

That win – a first against Mexico in the continental competition – sealed a place in the inter-confederation play-offs to keep alive their dreams of reaching Australia & New Zealand 2023.

< **63** >

D

⊕ DENMARK

Denmark are set to return to the FIFA Women's World Cup after an absence of 16 years. Quarter-final finishes in their first two outings remain the benchmark, but could a unified group of veterans, world stars and exciting youngsters be about to make their own mark?

COACH
LARS SØNDERGAARD

A midfielder in his playing days at AaB, the 64-year-old is a vastly experienced coach after decades in the men's Austrian *Bundesliga* and Danish *Superliga*, where he worked with a string of clubs. Brought into the national team set-up at the end of 2017 by former playing great Lene Terp, who was head of talent development at the Danish FA at the time. It was his first foray into women's football. Secured qualification for two major tournaments with unbeaten campaigns. In 2020 his contract was extended to take the team into 2023 and the FIFA Women's World Cup.

"We delivered a World Cup qualification that we can be really proud of," said Denmark's head coach Lars Søndergaard last September. "We are in a good place."

Booking an automatic ticket to this year's finals was a feat to relish, particularly as Denmark had missed out on three previous editions of the FIFA Women's World Cup in the play-offs. It was sweeter still given that the memory of losing to the Netherlands in their bid to reach France 2019 was still fresh for several players and their coach.

There was no heartache this time, as the high-scoring Danes were ahead in their qualifying group even before nearest rivals Russia were suspended. Closing out with a 5-1 win over Montenegro in Viborg, Denmark celebrated with their home fans with streamers, a giant "Down Under" banner and Danish beer.

They were rounding off a perfect campaign with eight wins in eight, 40 goals to the good and just two conceded. Perhaps as importantly, they were back to winning ways after failing to make it out of the "group of death" at the 2022 UEFA Women's EURO.

The Danes had been bullish on their way to qualifying for last summer's tournament, topping a

ABOVE: Mille Gejl celebrates another goal for her country – Denmark were prolific in qualifying.

< 64 >

tricky group, which included Italy, without losing a game. European Championship stalwarts, they had reached the semi-final stage six times previously.

When they arrived in England, however, they had even more to live up to – under former coach Nils Nielsen in 2017 an attack-minded group had made a historic run to the final. They lost out in a thriller with hosts the Netherlands, but had ended Germany's 22-year dominance of the competition along the way, and the gains that followed were palpable.

The national team went on to win a battle for improved pay and conditions; the eight-team domestic top flight has since garnered high-level sponsorship and TV coverage.

The women's side became part of the national consciousness too, and that was writ large in the run-up to the UEFA Women's EURO when they made their bow in the national stadium. A record 21,542 fans roared them on to a 2-1 win over Brazil in Copenhagen that night and scores of supporters would follow the team to England too.

What a team it was. Europe-based professionals such as Signe Bruun, Lene Christensen, Rikke Sevecke and Sofie Svava had all established themselves as key players in red and white under Søndergaard. At the forefront of the group were world-class forwards Pernille Harder and Nadia Nadim and the vastly experienced free-scoring Sanne Troelsgaard, all veterans of the 2017 campaign.

It was not to be, however. Germany took revenge with a 4-0 victory in their opener and, although Denmark kept their hopes alive by beating Finland

SIMONE BOYE SØRENSEN
BORN: 3 MARCH 1992
POSITION: DEFENDER

Denmark's player of the year in 2014, this cool and collected centre-back leads by example and always has the best interests of the team at heart. Missed EURO 2013 through injury but played every minute in their run to the 2017 EURO final, scoring the winning penalty in the semi-final shoot-out with Austria. Played college football in the USA before turning out for Brøndby, where she was captain, Rosengård, Bayern Munich and Arsenal, returning to Sweden with Hammarby in 2022. Has worked on the mental side of her game with a sports psychologist.

SIGNE BRUUN
BORN: 6 APRIL 1998
POSITION: FORWARD

This clinical striker made a scoring start within two minutes of her national-team debut in 2017. That same year she was named Female Talent of the Year as a rising star with Fortuna Hjørring. Has continued her upward trajectory at Paris Saint-Germain, with Olympique Lyonnais and on loan to Manchester United. Named Denmark's female footballer of the year in 2021, pipping Pernille Harder to the title. With 13 goals in seven games, she was Denmark's top scorer in FIFA Women's World Cup qualifiers. Has four younger brothers and describes her family as her "support system".

and went toe-to-toe with Spain, they were punished for missed chances by Marta Cardona's 90th-minute winner.

After his first major tournament with the women's side, Søndergaard took the positives as he looked towards the next: Australia & New Zealand 2023. "We have lifted our play, our morale, mentality, everything, since losing to Germany," he said. "We really showed we can play up against the best teams."

Now, an even stronger, wiser Denmark will look to do so again and to greater success against

the best in the world. They have the players to do it and, after so long away, the hunger too.

WOMEN'S WORLD CUP RECORD

1991	Quarter-finalists
1995	Quarter-finalists
1999	Group stage (4th)
2003	Did not qualify
2007	Group stage (3rd)
2011	Did not qualify
2015	Did not qualify
2019	Did not qualify

< 65 >

CHINA PR

In early 2022, the *Steel Roses* staged a string of stunning comebacks to claim a record-extending ninth continental crown and their first since 2006. Displaying a restored belief and fighting spirit, can this former powerhouse return to the top?

COACH
SHUI QINGXIA

A pioneer for the women's game in China PR, she has lived the sport's story in her country. A multiple winner of AFC Women's Asian Cup titles as a member of the "golden generation" across the 1980s and 1990s – she is yet to lose a game at the competition – she was also a silver medallist at the 1996 Olympic Games. Shui was the first Chinese woman to take the position of head coach and the first ex-international to do so. Having originally trained in athletics at sports school, Shui only started playing football aged 17. She was one of the first Chinese stars to play abroad, enjoying success in Japan with Suzuyo Shimizu FC Lovely Ladies in the L-League's heyday.

There was a wealth of positive reaction to China PR's gutsy 2022 AFC Women's Asian Cup triumph in India – and the resulting ticket to the FIFA Women's World Cup that it delivered. Cover shoots for fashion magazines, mass outpourings of praise across social media, a heroine's welcome in Suzhou, plus the 2022 National May 1st Labor Medal for coach Shui Qingxia and the National Worker Pioneer award for the team.

The celebratory scenes as the players tossed Shui into the air after their 3-2 final victory over Korea Republic revealed the squad's own euphoria at an astonishing turnaround in form by a side that had shown promise at the FIFA Women's World Cup

2019 before coming apart at the Olympic Games in 2021.

In France, they kept games tight and progressed out of a tough group including Germany and Spain before exiting in the round of 16, losing 2-0 against Italy. Two summers later in Japan, it was a different story, when the *Steel Roses* went down 5-0 to Brazil, drew 4-4 with newcomers Zambia and succumbed 8-2 to the Netherlands, results which ultimately forced the exit of coach Jia Xiuquan.

Ranked just fifth in Asia heading into the 2022 AFC Women's Asian Cup, the hosts of the first-ever edition of the FIFA Women's World Cup in 1991 and finalists in famous encounters against the USA in

ABOVE: China PR are nine-times AFC Women's Asian Cup champions and full of renewed confidence.

< 66 >

the 1996 Olympics and the FIFA Women's World Cup 1999 were seemingly still in the football doldrums.

New head coach Shui Qingxia would change all that, working on both the psychological and physical qualities of her squad.

The group stage went smoothly with a 4-0 win over Chinese Taipei and a 7-0 defeat of IR Iran securing their progress following the forced withdrawal of hosts India due to a number of positive COVID-19 cases. A quarter-final match-up with Vietnam proved less straightforward but, despite going behind early on, they recovered to dominate the game and prevail 3-1.

Reaching the final four in India had assured them of automatic qualification for Australia & New Zealand 2023.

Standing between them and a coveted place in the final were reigning champions Japan, and the old rivals served up a spectacular contest. Twice the *Nadeshiko* took the lead but the resilient *Steel Roses* levelled with just a minute of extra time remaining and displayed nerves of steel to win the resulting shoot-out 4-3.

A tenacious side that are typically hard to break down – favouring a 4-4-2 formation and aiming to quickly attack down the flanks and deliver crosses into the box – they faced a daunting 2-0 half-time deficit against Korea Republic in the final – their first since 2008. Encouraged by their coach to "fight for everyone watching back home", they regrouped and grabbed three goals, including a stoppage-time winner, in a gripping final 25 minutes to seal the sensational comeback.

Coach Shui has offered support to the growing cohort leaving the professional

ZHU YU
BORN: 23 JULY 1997
POSITION: GOALKEEPER

Named the AFC Women's Asian Cup 2022 goalkeeper of the tournament after her crucial saves in the two most high-pressure matches – keeping out Japan's first and fifth penalties in the 4-3 semi-final shoot-out win was huge. Basketball and badminton are other sports that she enjoys. Zhu actually started out as a defender but deputised in goal due to an injury to a team-mate and never looked back. An exciting new addition for Wuhan Jiangda when they got promoted to the Chinese Women's Super League in 2018, she was snapped up by WSL rivals Shanghai Shengli in March 2022.

WANG SHANSHAN
BORN: 27 JANUARY 1990
POSITION: DEFENDER/ FORWARD

Known as the "Nine-goal Diva" after netting nine times as a second-half substitute against Tajikistan at the 2018 Asian Games. The AFC Women's Asian Cup 2022 Most Valuable Player and, with Wang Shuang, her team's joint top scorer on five goals, two with either foot and one header. Brave in the air and comfortable both in defence and as a No. 9, she grabbed the late leveller and scored the winning penalty against Japan – and assisted Xiao Yuyi's championship winner. She was gifted one million Yuan by the provincial government as a reward.

Chinese Women's Super League to gain experience abroad, with *Steel Roses* seeing action at clubs across five leagues in Europe and playmaker Wang Shuang at Racing Louisville in the USA during 2022.

She has also called for calm and caution from supporters as they build towards a summer that

will include the delayed 2022 Asian Games on home soil, as well as the FIFA Women's World Cup 2023.

WOMEN'S WORLD CUP RECORD

1991	Quarter-finalists
1995	Fourth place
1999	Runners-up
2003	Quarter-finalists
2007	Quarter-finalists
2011	Did not qualify
2015	Quarter-finalists
2019	Round of 16

GROUP

E

🇺🇸 USA

The USA retained their FIFA Women's World Cup title at France 2019, serving up some sensational football along the way. The years since have been used to add more talent to the roster, but one objective remains — a unique hat-trick of consecutive crowns.

COACH
VLATKO ANDONOVSKI

Born in North Macedonia, he played for the national team's U-18s and as a professional for six years with three different clubs. Starred for a variety of sides in the Major Indoor Soccer League after moving to America and was twice named MISL All-Star. A tactically astute coach, the 46-year-old has won titles in youth soccer and the MISL as well as two National Women's Soccer League Championships with FC Kansas City. Twice named NWSL Coach of the Year, in 2019 he became the USA's ninth coach, enjoying the best start of any with 16 straight wins. Has led the USA to three SheBelieves Cups, Olympic bronze and the Concacaf W Championship title.

Original mentality monsters the USA arrived at the Concacaf W Championship in Mexico last summer as eight-time champions, having only ever conceded six goals, with one defeat and one draw along the way.

Predictably the favourites, they knew a top-two group-stage finish would land their ticket to the FIFA Women's World Cup; retaining the title would ensure an Olympic Games berth. Yet with Canada also among the eight nations in Monterrey, it would not be a procession.

At the Tokyo Games a year earlier, the *Canucks* had called time on a 20-year winless run against the USA by edging the semi-final. Canada would go on to claim gold, while the four-time Olympic champions got bronze.

Coming hot on the heels of a humbling 3-0 opening loss to Sweden in Tokyo Stadium, it was only the second defeat Vlatko Andonovski had tasted since taking over as USA head coach in October 2019.

A rebuild was underway, though, and even with the pandemic, by the close of 2021 Andonovski had called up 59 different players into training camps, giving 17 a first senior call-up and ten their debuts.

Ahead of the home SheBelieves Cup in 2022, eyebrows were raised when the coach opted for young prospects over seasoned performers, ten of his squad with

ABOVE: Back-to-back winners, the USA are focused on an unprecedented third title in a row.

fewer than 13 caps each. Rookies Catarina Macario, Margaret Purce, Ashley Sanchez and Sophia Smith rewarded his faith in crowd-pleasing wins over New Zealand and Iceland to retain the trophy.

Announcing his Concacaf squad that summer, the head coach spoke of hours spent evaluating match footage and in deep discussion with staff. Youngsters remained, but game-changing veterans had made the cut too.

Qualifying for Australia & New Zealand 2023 had proved straightforward enough, their mission complete after a 3-0 win over Haiti and five-goal rout of Jamaica. It would take a Kristie Mewis goal at the death to grind out a win over Mexico and they remained unbeaten after putting three past Costa Rica to reach the final.

There, they would meet Canada in a repeat of 2018. Now, as then, Alex Morgan was on the score-sheet, this time with a cool spot-kick winner against San Diego Wave team-mate Kailen Sheridan.

Morgan would depart with the Best Player Award; she, Lindsey Horan, Megan Rapinoe and captain Becky Sauerbrunn with a ringing endorsement from Andonovski. "We came out in the last game after being in a hotel for a month with the best energy that we've ever had," he said. "That's testament to, first and foremost, the senior players who were able to build a very good culture."

They would forge even closer bonds when a report into allegations of past abusive behaviour and sexual misconduct in women's professional soccer in the USA dropped just as they were embarking on a European tour. Unified, the USA went on to stand shoulder-to-shoulder with England to display a "protect the players" banner in front of 76,893 fans at Wembley Stadium.

Yet they would also suffer their first back-to-back losses since 2017, defeated in an end-to-end thriller by England before falling to Spain days later.

A raft of injuries was still hampering team selection as 2022 came to a close, but it meant chances for others and even the defeats were part of the learning process.

The USA are changing face but, with a mix of talented youngsters, experienced players and mercurial veterans, they are still surely the team to beat in 2023.

MALLORY SWANSON
BORN: 29 APRIL 1998
POSITION: FORWARD

Only 25 but a leader nevertheless, with more than 80 senior caps. With her quick feet and reading of the game, "Mal" creates goals and scores them too. Bounced back after a series of injuries to be named National Women's Soccer League MVP runner-up in 2021 and make the Best XI in 2022, with 11 goals and six assists for Chicago Red Stars. Kicked a ball as a kid with big sister Brianna in their yard. A Real Colorado youth product, she was just 17 when she scored on her national-team debut in 2016. Counts a goal at France 2019 and in the 2022 Concacaf semi-finals among her tally.

SOPHIA SMITH
BORN: 10 AUGUST 2000
POSITION: FORWARD

A lightning-fast and clinical attacker who has been scoring for fun since childhood, when she would travel for hours to attend training at Real Colorado. Scored 24 goals in 33 games at Stanford University, but left early to turn professional with Portland Thorns and has never looked out of place. Won the National Women's Soccer League Championship title in 2022 and, at 22, was the league's youngest-ever MVP. The US Soccer Young Female Player of the Year in 2017, in 2021 she was the first player born in 2000 to score for the senior team. Her motto is: "If you know better, do better".

WOMEN'S WORLD CUP RECORD

1991	Winners
1995	Third Place
1999	Winners
2003	Third Place
2007	Third Place
2011	Runners-up
2015	Winners
2019	Winners

< 69 >

⭐ VIETNAM

Appearing in their ninth consecutive AFC Women's Asian Cup, the *Golden Star Warriors* were the highest-ranked Asian side yet to reach a FIFA Women's World Cup. Having negotiated a serious COVID-19 outbreak, Vietnam will be looking to make their mark on the global stage.

COACH
MAI ĐỨC CHUNG

A former player for the General Department of Railways team, Chung's enormous coaching experience includes assistant, technical director and manager roles at club and national-team level, in men's and women's, youth and senior football in Vietnam. He first coached the women's national team in 1997 and has led them to five SEA Games successes, the first in 2003, during his four spells with the team. Lost weight and endured many sleepless nights due to the unprecedented pressures at the 2022 Asian Cup. Signed a new contract until the end of 2023 and, already in his 70s, he will be the elder statesman of the coaching cohort attending Australia & New Zealand 2023. Enjoys fishing in his spare time.

Vietnam went close to qualifying for the FIFA Women's World Cup 2015, but a 2-1 fifth-place play-off defeat meant Thailand were Canada-bound instead.

There was renewed optimism for the seven-time Southeast Asian Games gold medallists this time around, with eye-catching results in September 2021 in the qualifying tournament for the Asian Cup in India. They brushed aside the Maldives 16-0 and followed that with a 7-0 win over hosts Tajikistan. Pham Hai Yen, a four-time Vietnamese Women's National Championship top scorer, fired in eight goals in those two appearances.

Being drawn into the "group of death" for the Asian Cup seemed a slight setback but COVID-19 almost derailed their hopes entirely.

The squad headed to Spain at the end of December 2021 for a pre-tournament camp full of determination. Within two weeks, four players had contracted COVID-19 and, when the time came to fly to India, only six players, coach Mai Đức Chung and four staff made the flight.

Three further players fell ill on arrival and Chung was on the verge of asking the Vietnam Football Federation to withdraw the team. When 12 of the players still in Spain tested negative three days before the opening fixture, they were rushed onto a flight as soon as one became available.

ABOVE: Vietnam were overjoyed to qualify for their first global finals.

< 70 >

Having barely trained, Vietnam were pragmatic. The only side to play with a genuine sweeper in a back five at the tournament, they toughed out tricky ties against Korea Republic and Japan, holding both to 3-0 scorelines.

In the crucial third group game against Myanmar, Vietnam twice went behind but midfielder Nguyễn Thị Tuyết Dung's goal direct from a corner and a penalty from Huỳnh Nhu earned them a 2-2 draw.

With a goal difference superior to IR Iran's, they entered the knockout round as one of the two best third-place finishers.

2023 finals joint-host Australia's slightly unexpected loss to Korea Republic two hours before Vietnam's last-eight tie with China PR meant that the other three quarter-final losers would enter a round-robin to decide the one remaining automatic FIFA Women's World Cup spot.

Despite a 3-1 defeat to the Chinese, Chung highlighted this game as the turning point in their mood and fortunes.

Given his squad's understandable fatigue, the veteran coach told his players not to worry about the result, to avoid injury and disciplinary issues and use it as a rehearsal for the two repêchage play-off games against Thailand and Chinese Taipei.

The *Golden Star Warriors* took the game to a Thailand team still affected by their own COVID-19 outbreak and won 2-0.

Buoyed, Vietnam dominated possession against Chinese Taipei and, with the game at 1-1, Nguyễn Thị Bích Thủy controlled a lofted ball into the box on her right foot and smashed it home emphatically with her left. The final whistle was greeted with scenes of joy and the players' chants rang out around the empty DY Patil Stadium.

NGUYỄN THỊ BÍCH THỦY
BORN: 1 MAY 1994
POSITION: MIDFIELDER

Feisty, attack-minded midfielder who has a good on-field connection with Huỳnh Nhu having played together for club and country for so long. Joined Ho Chi Minh City in 2010 when invited by a coach who saw her playing at school. Missed the previous two AFC Women's Asian Cups through injury and two group games at the 2022 edition due to COVID-19. Scored the brilliantly taken, game-winning goal against Chinese Taipei in the play-off. Honoured in a ceremony by her local people's committee for her crucial contribution to the team's qualification, bringing joy to locals and inspiring youngsters in sport.

HUỲNH NHU
BORN: 28 NOVEMBER 1991
POSITION: FORWARD

Iconic and pioneering figure in the women's game in Vietnam, captain and all-time record scorer. Her lone strike defeated Thailand, in extra time, in the 2019 AFF Women's Championship final and her single goal also decided the 2021 SEA Games title, held in May 2022 against the same opposition. Four-time Vietnamese Golden Ball Footballer of the Year winner and recipient of numerous other individual accolades. Won seven national championships with Ho Chi Minh City. Signed one-year contract with Portuguese side Länk FC Vilaverdense in August 2022, the first Vietnamese woman to join a club in Europe.

President Nguyễn Xuân Phúc awarded them with medals and congratulated the team for making Vietnamese fans happy and proud.

The feel-good factor continued in May while retaining the SEA Games title on home soil and beating Thailand again in the process, though heavy defeats in France and to regional rivals Philippines in the AFF Women's Championship were sobering reminders of the work still to do ahead of their deserved arrival on the biggest stage.

WOMEN'S WORLD CUP RECORD

This will be Vietnam's first-ever appearance at the finals and they reached this historic milestone by beating Thailand 2-0 and Chinese Taipei 2-1 in a three-team repêchage play-off series at the 2022 AFC Women's Asian Cup.

< 71 >

⊜ NETHERLANDS

Former European champions and FIFA Women's World Cup finalists just four years ago, the *Oranje Leeuwinnen* are back with renewed focus and ambition. This proud footballing nation will endeavour to showcase the "Dutch way" to play at Australia & New Zealand 2023.

COACH
ANDRIES JONKER

A coach with a wealth of experience, including more than nine years as a leading technical coach and youth coordinator at the KNVB during the 1990s. Has operated as an assistant to Louis van Gaal at Barcelona and Bayern Munich, been academy manager at Arsenal, managed VfL Wolfsburg and coached at a number of Dutch clubs. Ended his three years as the boss at Telstar in the *Eerste Divisie* in the summer of 2022 to a round of applause in the dressing room. This is actually his second time at the reins of the *Oranje Leeuwinnen* after an interim spell in charge in 2001. Described as outspoken and self-confident, Jonker believes in the value of youth in football.

In 1971, the Netherlands and France featured in the first-ever FIFA recognised women's fixture but it was not until 2009 that the Dutch qualified for their first major tournament finals. They made it to the semi-finals of the continental championship on that occasion and qualified for the FIFA Women's World Cup 2015, but it was hosting and winning the UEFA Women's EURO 2017 that proved a watershed.

The nation was swept along on a tide of joyous orange during that home EURO, the players became household names and the *Oranje* Army continues to create a festive feel and follow the team in impressive numbers wherever they go.

The fans were out in force for the Netherlands' stirring run to the final of France 2019 and, although the team lost out to the USA, expectations for their further success have remained high.

It was a nerve-racking moment for the *Oranje Leeuwinnen* when they embarked on their final qualifier for Australia & New Zealand 2023. Needing to win their last match to avoid the play-offs, there was everything to play for against Iceland in Utrecht and the home side knew it, dominating a nervy encounter against a dogged opponent.

Denied by the woodwork, Iceland's superb shot-stopper Sandra Sigurðardóttir and a goal-line clearance, time was running

ABOVE: Finalists in 2019, the Netherlands edged Iceland in a tight qualifying group.

out until substitute Esmee Brugts swept in a cross in injury time that sailed into the goal to the absolute delight of a rocking crowd.

The Dutch were through with almost the very last kick in their final qualifier and, with Andries Jonker the new man at the helm, they could start looking forward.

Looking back, the Netherlands had enjoyed tremendous success under former coach Sarina Wiegman, who had taken them to two major finals and an Olympic quarter-final.

With their popular head coach already set to swap the Netherlands for England in the immediate aftermath of the Games, successful National Women's Soccer League coach Mark Parsons had been readied to take her place. Recruited from Portland Thorns in May 2021, Parsons had a contract until the end of the Australia & New Zealand 2023 qualifying campaign and including the 2022 UEFA Women's EURO.

Unfortunately for the reigning champions and their new English boss, injuries and COVID-19 cases in the camp would prove disruptive and depleting. Important players such as winger Lieke Martens, goal machine Vivianne Miedema and midfield engine Jackie Groenen were all affected and their EURO title defence was ended in a quarter-final extra-time exit at the boots of a superior France.

The Royal Dutch Football Association (KNVB) were unimpressed, describing the team's play and results as "disappointing" and Parsons exited shortly afterwards.

Brought in with very little time to prepare and with the crucial Iceland tie looming, the experienced Andries Jonker quickly drew a line under their recent championship chagrin, however.

DAPHNE VAN DOMSELAAR
BORN: 6 MARCH 2000
POSITION: GOALKEEPER

A string of outstanding performances made her an unexpected star of UEFA Women's EURO 2022 after replacing injured first-choice goalkeeper Sari van Veenendaal. Did not join a club until aged 11, and she enjoyed other sports, particularly volleyball. Signed for former Dutch champions FC Twente at 17, winning titles in 2019, 2021 and 2022. Made her debut and only pre-EURO appearance in a 3-0 win against Finland at the *Tournoi de France* in February 2022. Before France 2019, she was trying to fill her sticker book; this time she will hope to be in it.

JILL ROORD
BORN: 22 APRIL 1997
POSITION: MIDFIELDER

Fun-loving, technically adept midfielder from a sporty family; her father was a professional footballer and her mother played basketball. Long-time friend of Vivianne Miedema having been in teams together since she was 13, including the 2014 UEFA Women's U-19 Championship-winning side. Scored back-to-back hat-tricks for Arsenal in their opening two league fixtures in 2020. Has UEFA Women's Champions League experience with FC Twente, Bayern Munich, Arsenal and VfL Wolfsburg. Prefers the No. 10 role and arriving late into the box to provide a goalscoring threat.

"It's not about what happened," he said. "It's about what I think should be done. We have ambitious goals, but also an enormous amount of quality and talent that we can draw on for the 2023 World Cup."

Jonker knows Dutch football, the potential of the women's set-up, and its up-and-coming talent, having helped develop the youth structure in the country. He has also inherited a squad with experience – think double-centurion Sherida Spitse – and exciting younger potential like Lynn Wilms, Victoria Pelova, Fenna Kalma, Romée Leuchter and Brugts.

The *Oranje Leeuwinnen* were runners-up in 2019, so their target is to go one better in 2023.

WOMEN'S WORLD CUP RECORD

1991	Did not qualify
1995	Did not qualify
1999	Did not qualify
2003	Did not qualify
2007	Did not qualify
2011	Did not qualify
2015	Round of 16
2019	Runners-up

< 73 >

PORTUGAL

The top-ranked side at the inter-confederation play-offs, Portugal are building a reputation as one of the world's most exciting teams, and certainly impressed on their way to reaching February's tournament.

Portugal finished 2022 on a high after a year that had seen them play at a second UEFA Women's EURO and keep their dream of a first FIFA Women's World Cup berth alive.

Runners-up behind Germany in their qualifying group for this year's global finals, Portugal had scored 26 goals and lost just two matches, both against *Die Nationalelf*.

That meant they were still in with a chance of a place at Australia & New Zealand 2023 through the play-offs but, with fellow EURO 2022 outfit Belgium up first, it would not be easy.

Portugal were, though, buoyed by their own performances on the European stage that summer, a group with an average age of 26 having won praise for their technique, movement and high press.

They had come from behind to draw with Switzerland, and pulled two goals back in a 3-2 loss to the Netherlands before bowing out 5-0 to Sweden.

It was all valuable big-game experience and it came into play in the first round of European play-offs, with Fátima Pinto finally breaking down a strong Belgium side with a late headed winner to secure a 2-1 victory.

Even after being reduced to ten players, Iceland proved an even harder test in round two and it took extra-time goals from Diana Silva, Tatiana Pinto and Francisca Nazareth to complete a 4-1 win.

"Dreams are made to be fulfilled, and ours is so close!" declared the Portuguese FA in an excited statement on Twitter afterwards. It was true: the team were heading for February's inter-confederation play-offs and were just one win away from a first FIFA Women's World Cup.

COACH: FRANCISCO NETO

ONES TO WATCH:
FRANCISCA NAZARETH
BORN: 17 NOVEMBER 2002
POSITION: MIDFIELDER/ FORWARD

JÉSSICA SILVA
BORN: 11 DECEMBER 1994
POSITION: FORWARD

ABOVE: Proud Portugal are dreaming of a first FIFA Women's World Cup.
LEFT: Francisco Neto, head coach of Portugal.

< 74 >

★ CAMEROON

Cameroon powered to the round of 16 in the last two FIFA Women's World Cups with their flair, determination and attack-minded football.

COACH: GABRIEL ZABO

ONES TO WATCH:
AJARA NCHOUT
BORN: 12 JANUARY 1993
POSITION: FORWARD

GABRIELLE ONGUÉNÉ
BORN: 25 FEBRUARY 1989
POSITION: FORWARD

Debutants at the London 2012 Olympics but falling at the group stage, within three years Cameroon were forging their reputation at a first-ever FIFA Women's World Cup.

In Canada, they became only the second African team in the history of the competition to reach the knockout stages, a slender 1-0 round-of-16 loss to China PR ending their run.

Les Lionnes Indomptables made history at France 2019 as the first from their continent to get out of the group stage at two consecutive finals, England knocking them out in the second round.

A 1-0 quarter-final defeat by rivals Nigeria in last year's Women's Africa Cup of Nations saw them miss out on automatic qualification for a third finals on the bounce.

They clinched one of two coveted play-off spots, however, after beating Botswana 1-0 in repêchage thanks to a powerful long-range goal from Ajara Nchout.

LEFT: The Cameroon team, ready to face England at the FIFA Women's World Cup 2019.

✳

☰ THAILAND

An experienced Thailand team will be seeking a third consecutive FIFA Women's World Cup appearance when they take to the inter-confederation play-offs.

COACH: MIYO OKAMOTO

ONES TO WATCH:
SILAWAN INTAMEE
BORN: 22 JANUARY 1994
POSITION: MIDFIELDER

TANEEKARN DANGDA
BORN: 15 DECEMBER 1992
POSITION: FORWARD

As the most accomplished side in Southeast Asia – including five Southeast Asian Games and four AFF Women's Championship titles – the *Chaba Kaew* have competed at the last two editions of the global finals.

Unfortunately, a debilitating number of COVID-19 infections to key players around crucial encounters at the 2022 AFC Women's Asian Cup affected their attempts to qualify directly and make it three in a row.

Nine players were unavailable for their 7-0 quarter-final loss to Japan and another nine missed their first play-off match in the three-team round-robin repêchage for the final automatic spot.

Despite a brave effort, they went down 2-0 to Vietnam and then 3-0 in a pivotal tussle with Chinese Taipei.

Their squad is bolstered by a mix of exciting younger talent and multiple centurions with minutes at both Canada 2015 – where they beat Côte d'Ivoire 3-2 to finish third in their group – and France 2019.

LEFT: The Thailand team that met the *Matildas* in Melbourne in November 2022. They lost 2-0 in front of 11,271 fans.

< 75 >

FRANCE

France are set for a fifth appearance at the global finals, with their benchmark of success fourth place at Germany 2011. Now an exciting group are aiming to kick on in 2023 after reaching the semi-finals of last summer's UEFA Women's EURO.

COACH
CORINNE DIACRE

Just 14 when she first joined top-flight ASJ Soyaux, this former defender spent her senior club career there and was head coach for six years too. A legend for *Les Bleues*, she debuted aged 18, going on to captain her country and become the first to reach a century of caps. Scored in the play-off against England to help France reach their first FIFA Women's World Cup in 2003. Was assistant to then-head coach Bruno Bini in the 2011 edition when France achieved their best-ever finish of fourth. Spent three seasons as manager of men's professional Ligue 2 side Clermont Foot before joining France full-time in 2017, leading them to a first-ever UEFA Women's EURO semi-final in 2022.

A smiling France team took a leisurely lap of the pitch in Le Mans to applaud their tricolore-waving fans after securing their place at Australia & New Zealand 2023 last April. They had just beaten Slovenia 1-0 to record their eighth consecutive qualifying win and no team could catch them now, even with two games still to play.

There had been testing moments. Four days earlier, Wales had scored late on to set up an edgy finish in Llanelli and it had taken a 94th-minute penalty to beat Slovenia away.

A tap-in from the ever-lively Delphine Cascarino against Slovenia at home would maintain their winning momentum though, and their FIFA Women's World Cup ticket was assured.

The victory was head coach Corinne Diacre's 47th in 57 matches at the helm yet, while clearly joyful, the former France captain was nevertheless pragmatic. Theirs was not quite a "perfect" performance, but it was job done and the focus could now turn to the 2022 UEFA Women's EURO to come.

Les Bleues had a hoodoo to break in England that summer after having been knocked out at the quarter-final stage of their last five major tournaments, including France 2019.

The fallout from their last-eight exit on home soil three years previously was still being

ABOVE: Free-flowing France sealed qualification with two games to spare.

discussed as they headed across the Channel.

Some mainstays missed out, but Diacre said she believed it was important to regenerate the squad and she had to make difficult decisions. With almost half her line-up drawn from domestic giants Olympique Lyonnais and Paris Saint-Germain, and others playing at a high level in England, Italy and Spain, the squad was still strong.

Several fringe players at France 2019 had come into their own, including defender Sakina Karchaoui and midfielder Charlotte Bilbault. Left out in 2019, PSG's record goalscorer Marie-Antoinette Katoto was now shining for the national team. Forward Melvine Malard, midfielder Sandie Toletti, defender Selma Bacha and shot-stopper Pauline Peyraud-Magnin had also impressed.

With stalwart captain Wendie Renard leading them, all would feature at EURO 2022 as France blew Italy away 5-1 and reached the quarters with a tight 2-1 win over Belgium before a heavily changed side drew with Iceland.

A serious knee injury to pacy attacker Katoto took some of the gloss off, but full-back Ève Périsset helped secure a first semi-final berth on the European stage with a spot kick in extra time to beat the Netherlands.

A Wembley final was not to be, however, a Germany own goal and Diacre's tactical substitutions not enough to beat *Die Nationalelf* in a 2-1 loss watched by seven million on TV at home.

"We must remain united as we have done from the beginning, and stay together," was Diacre's clarion call afterwards.

Together again that September, two almost entirely different starting XIs beat Estonia and

GRACE GEYORO
BORN: 2 JULY 1997
POSITION: MIDFIELDER

An intelligent, incisive passer with an eye for goal, as a youth international she won gold in the FIFA U-17 Women's World Cup in 2012, silver in the U-20 edition in 2016 and was a UEFA Women's U-19 Championship winner that same year. Made history on her 50th cap in last summer's EURO by scoring a first-half hat-trick, a feat never before achieved in the European finals. A Paris Saint-Germain stalwart since the age of 15 and current captain, she won the league in 2020-21 and was named in the Trophées de D1, UNFP Trophées and UEFA Women's Champions League teams of the year.

SELMA BACHA
BORN: 9 NOVEMBER 2000
POSITION: DEFENDER

This outrageously skilful left-back plays with a confidence that belies her 22 years. Defensively solid, she can create goals too. Supplied the most assists in the 2021-22 UEFA Women's Champions League on the way to a remarkable fourth European title with Olympique Lyonnais since the age of 17. Named the competition's Young Player of the Season. Joined OL as an eight-year-old and started her international career with the U-16s, winning the UEFA Women's U-19 Championship in 2019 and making her senior debut two years later. Player of the match in France's 2022 UEFA Women's EURO quarter-final.

Greece to end FIFA Women's World Cup qualifying with a perfect 10 wins, 54 goals scored and four conceded.

Seeing influential defender Griedge Mbock join Katoto on the long-term injury list during that camp was less positive. Losing the high-intensity friendlies with Germany and Sweden that followed were tests of France's resolve too.

Yet with time still on their side and friendlies against other top opponents in the calendar to bolster their experience in the run-up, the highly technical,

ambitious and attack-minded *Les Bleues* will be a contest for any team on this world stage.

WOMEN'S WORLD CUP RECORD

1991	Did not qualify
1995	Did not qualify
1999	Did not qualify
2003	Group stage (3rd)
2007	Did not qualify
2011	Fourth place
2015	Quarter-finalists
2019	Quarter-finalists

< 77 >

JAMAICA

Jamaica deserved all the plaudits when they qualified for France 2019 after a tumultuous few years in the wilderness. They would have to rally to repeat the feat, but they did so and in style, beating the odds to make history yet again.

COACH
LORNE DONALDSON

Former Jamaica international who made his debut aged 17. Moved to the USA in 1980 and was a three-time All-American and the first footballer to make the Metro State College hall of fame. Won two American Professional Soccer League championships as a coach at men's side Colorado Foxes. Real Colorado's executive director of coaching, he is widely respected for his work with the club since the late 1990s, bringing through USA stars like Mallory Swanson and Sophia Smith. Named United Soccer Coaches national coach of the year for youth girls in 2017 while also leading Jamaica's U-20s. Assisted Hue Menzies at France 2019 and had previously served as interim head coach before taking the top job in June 2022.

The *Reggae Girlz* were the toast of Jamaica in 2018 when a qualification campaign inspired by Khadija "Bunny" Shaw saw them become the first Caribbean nation to reach the FIFA Women's World Cup.

In 2022, they knew they would need every ounce of Shaw's goalscoring prowess and a huge squad effort to reach the global finals for a second time on the bounce.

Four automatic spots for Australia & New Zealand 2023 were on offer at the Concacaf W Championship and Jamaica were pitched into a group with opponents they had yet to beat at the continental finals. Head coach Lorne Donaldson had only been appointed five weeks beforehand, so preparation time was tight.

It was just another challenge for Jamaica's women, who had gone through a turbulent time since late 2019, having no competitive fixtures for 16 months during the pandemic and with two coaches coming and going.

Government help had been needed to fund flights to Grenada during their qualifying campaign in early 2022, but they had finished top of the group with four wins from four to secure a seventh Concacaf championship appearance since 1991.

Arriving in Mexico for Donaldson's first match in charge, a squad that included 12 from France

ABOVE: Four years on from their finals debut, Jamaica continue to flourish.

< 78 >

2019 and a host of new faces knew they would have their work cut out against the hosts, three times their conquerors in this competition previously.

They had to hang on after a Shaw header from Deneisha Blackwood's free kick put them into an early lead, but 'keeper Becky Spencer stood tall and, despite a missed penalty from Havana Solaun, scorer of their only goal at France 2019, the win was theirs.

Facing Concacaf and world champions the USA in the subsequent match, they were humbled 5-0 so, with their next opponents Haiti having also beaten Mexico, it was all to play for.

Their better goal difference meant a draw would suffice for Haiti, who also had the historical edge of two previous finals victories over the *Reggae Girlz*. With a ticket to the FIFA Women's World Cup riding on the outcome, it would be quite the test.

Qualifying goal-getters Trudi Carter and Shaw put Jamaica in the driving seat before the hour, but Haiti kept on coming, denied by the post and former England youth shot-stopper Spencer.

A Shaw spot kick after a handball in the area would ease the pressure, before another ex-England recruit, Drew Spence, sealed the win, sparking joyous celebrations on the pitch as the players danced and scampered around with the Jamaican flag aloft.

They went on to suffer semi-final defeat to Canada, but an extra-time goal from substitute Kalyssa Van Zanten against Costa Rica secured third place and an Olympic play-off spot.

Back in 2008, the Jamaican team stopped playing because of a lack of funds, only returning six years later after a rescue package from

KHADIJA SHAW
BORN: 31 JANUARY 1997
POSITION: MIDFIELDER/FORWARD

Jamaica's all-time leading goalscorer, this Spanish Town native had represented every youth level, including the U-20s, by the age of 14. Made a scoring debut for the seniors at 18, her goals since helping Jamaica qualify for consecutive FIFA Women's World Cups. A University of Tennessee player at France 2019, she graduated with a degree in communications and a raft of personal awards. At Bordeaux she was *Division 1 Féminine* top scorer with 22 goals in 20 matches and made the team of 2020-21. Won the League Cup in her first season at Manchester City.

DREW SPENCE
BORN: 23 OCTOBER 1992
POSITION: MIDFIELDER

This Londoner changed sporting nationality from England in 2021 but is already part of Jamaica's history after scoring against Haiti to help secure FIFA Women's World Cup qualification. Made the Concacaf W Championship Best XI and it is easy to see why with her ability not just to score, but break up play and set attacks in motion. Signed for English Women's Super League side Tottenham Hotspur in 2022 following a remarkable 14-year career at Chelsea, where she won 11 major trophies. Probably one of the most understated players in the English league, she brings a winning mentality and professionalism to any team.

Cedella Marley, the daughter of reggae legend Bob.

While the 2018 achievement of securing a first FIFA Women's World Cup berth was remarkable, doing it again has been no mean feat either.

Yet while challenges remain, the *Reggae Girlz* will face this tournament with more depth and experience than ever before. The majority of the squad compete at a high level as professionals in the UK and USA and, before 2022 was out, Donaldson had already started to explore the team's identity and style of play.

The journey continues now for Jamaica. Who knows what they can achieve in 2023?

WOMEN'S WORLD CUP RECORD

1991	Did not qualify
1995	Did not qualify
1999	Did not enter
2003	Did not qualify
2007	Did not qualify
2011	Did not enter
2015	Did not qualify
2019	Group stage (4th)

< 79 >

BRAZIL

Brazil are FIFA Women's World Cup ever-presents, former finalists and the dominant force in the women's game in South America. But are the current *Seleção* ready to step out from the shadow of former greats and fight again for global success?

COACH
PIA SUNDHAGE

A true legend of the women's game, as a girl she called herself Pelé and dreamt of being a footballer. Made her international debut aged 15 and went on to be the first Swedish woman to gain 100 caps. Won gold at the inaugural European Championship in 1984, plus bronze at the first-ever FIFA Women's World Cup in 1991. Famous for bursting into song and serenading players and the press alike, her vast coaching résumé includes clubs in Sweden and America then Olympic gold in 2008 and 2012 plus silver at the FIFA Women's World Cup 2011 with the USA. She also led Sweden to silver at the Rio 2016 Olympics before taking up the challenge of managing Brazil in July 2019.

Brazil's 2022 *Copa América Femenina* triumph saw them claim their eighth South American crown in its ninth edition and sealed their place at Australia & New Zealand 2023 and the 2024 Paris Olympics too.

After defeating Argentina, Uruguay, Venezuela, Peru and then Paraguay in the semi-final, they faced Colombia in July's final. They went ahead with a 39th-minute penalty and held on stoutly to win 1-0, despite the efforts of the spirited hosts and a sold-out, partisan home crowd in Bucamaranga. It was Debinha's deft touch and body movement that drew the foul in the box and she sent the goalkeeper the wrong way from the resultant spot kick.

One goal proved sufficient for a well-drilled and efficient Brazil side that closed out the tournament having scored 20 and conceding none. Lorena's six clean sheets meant they were the first team to successfully shut out every opponent for the entire competition.

Their fourth successive South American crown confirmed Swede Pia Sundhage as the first female coach to lift the trophy and earned the *Seleção* $1.5 million in prize money too.

These accomplishments were also notable considering they were achieved without Formiga, Cristiane or Marta, Brazil's first major tournament appearance not involving at least one of the

ABOVE: Can Brazil finally turn South American dominance into success on the world stage?

iconic and influential trio since early 1995.

A refresh of the squad had been inevitable given that the average age at the FIFA Women's World Cup 2019 was 28 years and five months, the tournament's all-time third-oldest squad.

They finished third in their group in France, then lost out to the hosts 2-1 in the round of 16 – the same stage they had exited in 2015 – and veteran coach Vadão was replaced by Sundhage shortly afterwards.

The Swedish coach knows through first-hand experience with the USA and Sweden that medal-winning success can take time. As she likes to keep in mind: "Winning a title is not a 100-metre sprint."

So the operation of rebuilding and tweaking the team's style of play in preparation for 2023 began immediately after the Tokyo Games in 2021, where they remained unbeaten but went out to eventual champions Canada in the quarter-finals after losing on penalties.

Confident that her side contains ample skill and pace, Sundhage has focused on cementing the team's cohesion and thoughtfully integrating talented youngsters.

Chief among the new faces are stars of Brazil's FIFA U-20 Women's World Cup 2022 bronze medal-winning side such as exciting midfielder Yaya, solid defender Lauren and her fellow centre-back Tarciane, recipient of the Bronze Ball for the tournament's third-best player.

The *Seleção* have remained ninth or higher in the FIFA/Coca-Cola Women's World Ranking since December 2019, after an earlier dip outside of the top ten and, after their *Copa América Femenina* winning streak, went on to beat South Africa, Norway and Italy in friendlies before 2022 was out – all signposts of positive progress.

Hopefully, Marta – arguably the

RAFAELLE
BORN: 18 JUNE 1991
POSITION: DEFENDER

Left-footed ball-playing central defender, strong in the air and can play up front too – she became leading scorer for the University of Mississippi with 44 goals in three years. Having featured for the *Seleção* in two Olympic Games and two *Copa América Femenina* campaigns, this will be her second FIFA Women's World Cup after an ACL injury kept her out of France 2019. Was made captain in Marta's absence and said lifting the *Copa América* trophy was a "dream come true". Spent six seasons with Changchun in the Chinese Women's Super League before joining English outfit Arsenal in January 2022.

ADRIANA
BORN: 17 NOVEMBER 1996
POSITION: FORWARD

Gained the nickname "Maga", or "Sorceress", for her craftiness and creativity. Has won multiple league titles, as well as the *Copa Libertadores Femenina* with Brazil's most successful club Corinthians. Grabbed five goals at last year's *Copa América Femenina*, her major tournament debut, having missed the FIFA U-20 Women's World Cup 2016 and the Tokyo Olympics through injury as well as France 2019 after rupturing her ACL the day before the squad assembled. Has joked that if she had not played football in their town of União, none of the local children could have – her dad owned the ball and the field where they played.

greatest woman ever to play the game – recovers from the ACL injury she suffered in March 2022 and returns for Australia & New Zealand 2023 to extend her record of 17 goals over five successive FIFA Women's World Cups. She will be 37 by July 2023, however, so while this living legend can still inspire, she may no longer be expected to dominate games or inject the same level of energy as in competitions gone by.

Sundhage can look to others, like experienced defenders Rafaelle and Tamires, and resourceful forwards Debinha and Bia

Zaneratto, to drive her side towards success.

WOMEN'S WORLD CUP RECORD

1991	Group stage (3rd)
1995	Group stage (4th)
1999	Third place
2003	Quarter-finalists
2007	Runners-up
2011	Quarter-finalists
2015	Round of 16
2019	Round of 16

< 81 >

CHINESE TAIPEI

A historic powerhouse in the early years of the women's game in Asia, Chinese Taipei were participants in the inaugural FIFA Women's World Cup.

COACH: YEN SHIH-KAI

ONES TO WATCH:
CHEN YEN-PING
BORN: 20 AUGUST 1991
POSITION: FORWARD

SU SIN-YUN
BORN: 20 NOVEMBER 1996
POSITION: DEFENDER

LEFT: Lai Li-chin celebrates with her team-mates after scoring at the 2022 AFC Women's Asian Cup.

After a hat-trick of Asian Cup titles a decade earlier, Chinese Taipei lost to Italy and Germany but beat Nigeria 2-0 to make the last eight at those maiden global finals in 1991, losing 7-0 to eventual champions the USA.

Absent from the AFC Women's Asian Cup since 2008 and playing a direct style of football under then-coach Kazuo Echigo, a crucial 5-0 triumph over IR Iran at the 2022 iteration set up a quarter-final tie against the Philippines for a place at this FIFA Women's World Cup. Zhuo Li-Ping's superb 82nd-minute equaliser took the encounter to extra time but they lost the shoot-out and thus entered the three-team play-off for the remaining direct qualifying place.

The *Blue Magpies*, as they are unofficially known, defeated Thailand 3-0 and only needed to avoid defeat against Vietnam to grab the fifth automatic spot but were edged 2-1 in a thrilling contest.

Ambitions for Australia & New Zealand 2023 now rest with the inter-confederation play-offs.

---

*

PARAGUAY

Paraguay were the surprise package at the *Copa América Femenina* 2022 in Colombia and were proud to finish in South America's top four.

COACH: MARCELLO FRIGÉRIO

ONES TO WATCH:
RAMONA MARTÍNEZ
BORN: 21 JULY 1996
POSITION: MIDFIELDER

JESSICA MARTÍNEZ
BORN: 14 JUNE 1999
POSITION: FORWARD

LEFT: Paraguay's players pose ahead of their 2022 *Copa América Femenina* first-round tie against Chile.

The critical missing piece from an otherwise positive continental championship for Paraguay was a ticket to Australia & New Zealand 2023.

After losing to the hosts, they defeated Chile, Bolivia and Ecuador in the group stage and guaranteed their spot at the 2023 Pan American Games in Chile.

Eventual champions Brazil beat them 2-0 in the semi-final, which led to a crunch decider against Argentina for third place and a coveted qualifying berth for the global finals. They were on top until *La Albiceleste* hit back to win 3-1 late on.

Robert Harrison, president of the Paraguayan Football Association, hailed the team's efforts in Colombia as "just the beginning".

Regular training camps and practice fixtures throughout 2022 ensured preparation for the inter-confederation play-offs continued with focus.

They are a close-knit unit that have grown up together and, with the bulk of the regular squad playing abroad in Argentina, Brazil, Chile, Portugal, Spain and Türkiye, they are determined to succeed.

< 82 >

PAPUA NEW GUINEA

The "football queens of the Pacific", Papua New Guinea are five-time Pacific Games gold medallists and the current OFC Women's Nations Cup champions.

COACH: SPENCER PRIOR

ONES TO WATCH:
YVONNE GABONG
BORN: 29 AUGUST 1996
POSITION: MIDFIELDER

RAMONA PADIO
BORN: 13 MARCH 1998
POSITION: MIDFIELDER

In the absence of the *Football Ferns* at last year's continental finals, and after three previous second-place finishes, Papua New Guinea's players rose to the occasion, dealt with the weight of expectation and finally claimed the Oceania title.

Utilising their pace and togetherness, they beat Vanuatu 3-1, Tahiti 2-1, Tonga on penalties after a 3-3 draw, Samoa 3-0 in the semi-final and then hosts Fiji 2-1 in the final.

Meagen Gunemba and Ramona

LEFT: Papua New Guinea made history by winning the OFC Women's Nations Cup in 2022.

Padio were joint top scorers in Fiji with five each.

Qualifying for the FIFA Women's World Cup is the ultimate dream and the route for the Nations Cup victors is via the inter-confederation play-offs.

Winning coach Nicola Demaine was released and a number of players did not train for some time, which stalled momentum.

Results dropped off too, with goalless losses to Fiji, the Solomon Islands and Philippines in November and December before former men's professional Spencer Prior was installed with just three months to prepare the team.

---

*

PANAMA

Panama have yet to appear at a FIFA Women's World Cup but they have previously come within touching distance of a maiden berth via the play-offs.

COACH: IGNACIO QUINTANA

ONES TO WATCH:
YENITH BAILEY
BORN: 29 MARCH 2001
POSITION: GOALKEEPER

MARTA COX
BORN: 20 JULY 1997
POSITION: MIDFIELDER

Five years ago, Panama suffered the agony of missing out on France 2019 after losing 4-0 away then drawing 1-1 at home to Argentina in the inter-confederation play-off.

They were assured of the chance to go again in 2023 after finishing third in their group at last summer's Concacaf W Championship, courtesy of a Marta Cox goal against Trinidad and Tobago.

It was one of several successes in 2022. On the way to qualifying

LEFT: Panama's players prepare to face Canada at the 2022 Concacaf W Championship.

for the continental finals, *Las Canaleras* recorded four consecutive wins, scoring 24 goals without reply – all new experiences for Panama.

By the close of the year, they had beaten Ecuador 1-0 to record their maiden win over a South American team, going on to draw with them before beating Venezuela too.

It was their longest consecutive unbeaten run against South American opposition and viewed as a sign of Panama's progress.

< 83 >

⊕ SWEDEN

The *Blågult* collected Olympic silver medals in 2016 and 2021 and bagged bronze at the FIFA Women's World Cup 2019. The squad has the quality and the hunger to succeed. Is now the time that Sweden finally turn their experience and guile into gold?

COACH
PETER GERHARDSSON

Former striker and Swedish youth international who worked as a police officer for spells alongside his playing career. Scored 49 top-flight goals during his time with Hammarby IF. Has coached men's and women's sides, starting out with hometown club Upsala IF. Guided Gothenburg-based men's team BK Häcken to an *Allsvenskan* runners-up spot in 2012 and a first-ever Swedish Cup win in 2016, and was brought in to take charge of the *Blågult* after EURO 2017. He is a massive music fan and feels it is an important part of his everyday and footballing life: it helps with relaxation and match preparation.

Kosovare Asllani's second-half leveller against the Republic of Ireland in April 2022 saw Sweden secure their spot at Australia & New Zealand 2023, becoming the first European side to do so. The talismanic playmaker's goal had earned a deserved draw in the home tie against the Irish, Group A's eventual runners-up.

The match marked the only dropped points in a steady campaign that included three wins by one-goal margins – against Slovakia, Republic of Ireland and Finland – and some sizeable score-lines, including 15-0 against Georgia.

Sweden have been proudly ever-present at every FIFA Women's World Cup finals and only failed to progress past the group stage once in nearly 30 years, at China PR 2007.

The tense semi-final at France 2019 went to extra time before the Netherlands edged it and a crowd of 30,000 received them in Gothenburg on their return, showing their appreciation for the team's efforts in beating England to take third place.

After sweeping aside world champions USA 3-0 in the opener at the Tokyo Olympics and impressing with their positive and attack-minded performances, it was only the stubbornly defensive Canadians and a wayward spot kick by Europe's all-time most-capped player Caroline Seger that saw them head home with silver and not gold.

ABOVE: Sweden won bronze in 2019, silver in 2021 and seek gold in 2023.

Sweden spent the next 12 months between August 2021 and 2022 ranked second in the world, having won the 2022 Algarve Cup and remained unbeaten since March 2020, the penalty shoot-out in the Olympic final aside.

On the back of that form, they headed to the UEFA Women's EURO 2022 with high expectations and a record 33,218 fans flocked to Solna to watch their 3-1 comeback against Brazil in a send-off fixture.

Unfortunately, injuries and COVID-19 cases disrupted their line-ups in England and the *Blågult* never quite hit their groove. They were severely punished for wasting chances in the opening half-hour against England in the semi-final, going on to lose by a bruising 4-0, equalling their heaviest-ever defeat.

The focus turned to Australia & New Zealand 2023 and the ambition to reach a first FIFA Women's World Cup final since 2003.

The *Damallsvenskan* is no longer a draw for the world's best players in the way that it was during the 2000s, and so many of Sweden's players have moved abroad where there are obvious gains to be had.

Exciting Swedish exports, like midfielders Hanna Bennison, Filippa Angeldahl and Johanna Rytting Kanerydm, and forwards Stina Blackstenius and Lina Hurtig, all played in the English Women's Super League in 2022-23.

Established stars Magdalena Eriksson of Chelsea and Fridolina Rolfö at FC Barcelona get to train daily alongside and opposite the world's best, like Sam Kerr of Australia and Spain's Alexia Putellas.

Peter Gerhardsson has cultivated

MAGDALENA ERIKSSON
BORN: 8 SEPTEMBER 1993
POSITION: DEFENDER

A defensive rock and inspirational leader, Eriksson can play centrally or at full-back and has a huge determination to win. An important cog in Sweden's 2012 UEFA Women's U-19 Championship triumph as well as Linköpings FCs' table-topping, unbeaten league campaign in 2016. Won the Women's Super League title four times in her first five years after joining Chelsea in 2017. Was made the *Blues*' captain in the 2019-20 season and won Sweden's prestigious player of the year *Diamantbollen* in 2020. Studied political science and feminist theory. Taught herself to play guitar with YouTube videos.

FRIDOLINA ROLFÖ
BORN: 24 NOVEMBER 1993
POSITION: FORWARD

Powerful, pacy, left-footed forward who can play wide or through the middle. Another 2012 U-19 European champion, double Olympic silver medallist and France 2019 bronze medallist. "Frido" grew up admiring Brazil's midfield maestro Marta. Won the *Damallsvenskan* with Linköpings FC in 2016, and finished runner-up in the *Frauen-Bundesliga* for three consecutive seasons after joining Bayern Munich in January 2017 before finally earning a winners' medal with VfL Wolfsburg in 2020. Signed for FC Barcelona in July 2021 and twice named *Diamantbollen* as Sweden's female player of the year.

a welcoming and accepting environment in which players feel the freedom to be themselves and actively look forward to being on international duty. This culture reflects the positive attitude he asks for on the pitch too, wanting players to be brave, physically strong, aggressive and to think about what they can do with the ball, not without it.

Sweden have become a unit that can be flexible with their formation and attacking options, though set pieces remain important too: defenders contributed 25 per cent of their

goals in EURO 2022 qualifying.

The *Blågult* are a tournament team who play to win.

WOMEN'S WORLD CUP RECORD

1991	Third place
1995	Quarter-finalists
1999	Quarter-finalists
2003	Runners-up
2007	Group stage (3rd)
2011	Third place
2015	Round of 16
2019	Third place

< **85** >

🇿🇦 SOUTH AFRICA

South Africa endured a baptism of fire up against Spain, China PR and Germany in their maiden FIFA Women's World Cup four years ago. Winless, they still left with heads held high. This time out, the first–time African champions are aiming to get points on the board.

COACH
DESIREE ELLIS

An inspirational figure at home and abroad for her exploits as both a player and coach, Ellis is the only South African to win the COSAFA Women's Championship wearing both hats and hit a hat-trick in South Africa's first international in 1993. After retiring in 2002, she went on to coach her former team, Cape Town-based Spurs. Joined *Banyana Banyana*'s coaching staff as an assistant in 2014. As interim, then head coach, since 2016 the 60-year-old has led South Africa to four COSAFA titles, the historic WAFCON win and consecutive FIFA Women's World Cups. A three-time African Women's Coach of the Year winner, she is also a FIFA mentor.

South Africa arrive at Australia & New Zealand 2023 wearing a new crown: that of Women's Africa Cup of Nations champions. Five times *Banyana Banyana* had reached the final of their continental championship in the past and on every occasion they returned home with runners-up medals but never the trophy.

All that changed in July 2022 when, after a gripping final against hosts Morocco that was watched by millions on television and thousands more in the stands, they at last emerged victorious.

Only the third nation to win the title in the competition's history, they also secured a second consecutive FIFA Women's World Cup berth along the way, all while overcoming a COVID-19 outbreak and the loss of their star player.

It was an achievement that head coach Desiree Ellis, who played for South Africa in a losing final against Nigeria in 2000, would later describe as "huge". "It's not only changed the narrative for women's football, but for women's sport," Ellis said, adding that she hoped more sponsors and media coverage would follow.

The new "Queens of Africa" warranted it after WAFCON. For starters, they had to get out of a group that included Botswana, who, in 2019, had ended South

ABOVE: South Africa were victorious at the 2022 Women's Africa Cup of Nations.

< 86 >

Africa's bid to reach a third consecutive Olympic Games, and Nigeria, their victors in the 2018 WAFCON final on penalties.

The squad that Ellis had assembled for the tournament was a strong one. Overseas stars Thembi Kgatlana, Hildah Magaia, Linda Motlhalo and Jermaine Seoposenwe were at the forefront. Italy-based Refiloe Jane, veteran defender Janine van Wyk and 2021 CAF Women's Champions League-winning Mamelodi Sundowns 'keeper, Andile Dlamini, all shared the armband. Ellis also included a sports psychologist in her backroom staff.

They enjoyed a dream start, with goals from Seoposenwe and Magaia putting Nigeria to bed in the opener. Debutants Burundi were beaten 3-1 in the game that followed. Botswana were edged out 1-0, although it was not a victory without cost as star forward Kgatlana suffered a tournament-ending Achilles rupture in the process.

Hit by a COVID-19 outbreak ahead of a crunch quarter-final with Tunisia that would decide their FIFA Women's World Cup fate, they battled on to win 1-0.

South Africa had taken one of four automatic tickets for Australia & New Zealand and an emotional Ellis hailed her team and staff, dedicating their success to everyone at home.

The pride of their nation would know no bounds when, having edged out Zambia in the semi-final on Mandela Day, a brace from Magaia helped beat Morocco to take the title in Rabat.

Just over a month later, U-17 coach Simphiwe Dludlu led a fringe *Banyana Banyana* side to runners-up medals in the COSAFA Women's Championship for southern African nations. It was a chance to hand youngsters

JERMAINE SEOPOSENWE
BORN: 12 OCTOBER 1993
POSITION: FORWARD

Played in a Cape Town boys' team before her first foray into women's football at Santos Ladies. In 2010, aged just 16, she became the first South African to score in any FIFA women's finals tournament after netting in the U-17 edition. Ever-present at the Olympic Games in 2016, she came off the bench twice at France 2019. Named in the WAFCON Best XI, she was praised for her decision-making and eye for goal. A Portuguese Cup winner with Sporting Braga, she joined FC Juárez in 2022, going on to bag the fastest goal in the history of the Mexican top flight.

THEMBI KGATLANA
BORN: 2 MAY 1996
POSITION: FORWARD

The first South African to score at a senior FIFA Women's World Cup with a wonderful goal against Spain at France 2019. Went into the tournament as reigning African Women's Player of the Year having finished as leading scorer and player of the tournament at WAFCON 2018. Had to support the 2022 WAFCON title win from the sidelines after an Achilles injury in the group stage, celebrating on her crutches in the final. Has played top-flight football in the USA, China PR, Portugal and Spain. A talented professional, she also runs her own non-profit foundation to support and bring on female footballers.

tournament experience, with Ellis looking to expand her player pool before slimming it down to the final squad for Australia & New Zealand 2023.

The core of the group remains, of course, and, with so many now playing abroad as professionals, widening their competitive nous in the process, the levels will only rise.

Friendly defeats to the Netherlands, Brazil and Australia in 2022 showed that there is still work to do in the face of top opponents, but this is an ambitious football nation and,

when the time comes, they will want to show the world what they are capable of.

WOMEN'S WORLD CUP RECORD

1991	Did not enter
1995	Did not qualify
1999	Did not qualify
2003	Did not qualify
2007	Did not qualify
2011	Did not qualify
2015	Did not qualify
2019	Group stage (4th)

< 87 >

ITALY

Italy departed the FIFA Women's World Cup four years ago to a standing ovation. Quarter-finalists then, can *Le Azzurre* light up the tournament again in their first-ever back-to-back finals appearance?

COACH
MILENA BERTOLINI

This Italian Hall of Famer won multiple domestic titles in 15 seasons as a defender in Italy's *Serie A* and continued in the same vein as a top-flight coach first with Foroni Verona, then Reggiana and Brescia. Took Brescia to the UEFA Women's Champions League quarter-finals in 2016. Winner of six "Golden Bench" coach of the year gongs and only the second Italian woman to gain the UEFA Pro Licence, she was appointed Italy boss in 2017 and led them to a first FIFA Women's World Cup quarter-final berth since 1991. A clever tactician who instils confidence, the 57-year-old will aim to get Italy back on track at this year's finals after a disappointing UEFA Women's EURO 2022 campaign.

After an absence of 20 years from the world stage, Italy shone in 2019, a mostly amateur side impressing with their technical flair and celebratory renditions of the "Macarena". With a total of more than 24 million viewers in Italy avidly tuning into their five matches, *Le Azzurre*'s next major outing, at the UEFA Women's EURO 2022, was eagerly anticipated.

European Championship runners-up in 1993 and 1997, Italy had been ever-present at every subsequent EURO. They barely got off the ground in England. Stunned by a 5-1 opening loss to France, they would draw with Iceland and push Belgium to the limit, but exit early with a single point and two goals to their name.

Clearly disappointed, head coach Milena Bertolini was nevertheless pragmatic, marking the experience down as one they could learn and eventually derive strength from.

A quick recovery was vital with the last two UEFA qualifiers for Australia & New Zealand 2023 just around the corner. It had been an almost perfect campaign, but a home loss to Switzerland in November 2021 had meant that a mere two points were all that separated

ABOVE: Italy celebrate their first-ever consecutive FIFA Women's World Cup finals ticket.

< 88 >

Italy from their nearest rivals.

Ahead of their visit to Moldova – her 60th match at the helm – Bertolini revealed that she had worked to move staff and players on from their EURO disappointment. "We start again with confidence," she added. "I told the girls that we have to be hungry, to show what we're capable of."

With skipper Sara Gama joining an injury list that included Valentina Bergamaschi and Barbara Bonansea, Cristiana Girelli would captain Italy to a thumping 8-0 win in Chișinău.

Four days later, a largely unchanged first XI faced world No. 40 side Romania in front of 3,000 supporters at Ferrara's Stadio Paolo Mazza. The previous summer, Italy had beaten their France 2019 quarter-final victors, the Netherlands, in a friendly at the Mazza, and they were yet to lose there.

Yet with so much at stake, the hosts made a nervy start, only settling into the tie when AS Roma's new signing Valentina Giacinti drilled home a left-footed strike on the half-hour. With goals raining in as Switzerland dominated Moldova in Lausanne, Italy needed to put their own qualifier to bed. Lisa Boattin did so in the 74th minute, her long-distance wonder-shot sending Italy to consecutive FIFA Women's World Cup finals for an historic first-ever time.

"We were really down and disappointed about how things worked out in England," Bertolini would say later. "We wanted to show that wasn't who we are. When you qualify in the way that we did, you can only feel pleased about it."

With many having been part of EURO 2022, the tears at full

CRISTIANA GIRELLI
BORN: 23 APRIL 1990
POSITION: FORWARD

A highly competitive and prolific striker who is known for her aerial prowess, she played against boys until she was 14. In over a decade with the national team, she has featured in three EUROs and hit a hat-trick against Jamaica at France 2019. Known as "Chef" for her love of cooking, she is a fluent English speaker. She has won multiple *Scudetti* and Italian Cups, carving her name into Juventus' history in 2021 as the first player to score a half-century of goals for the club. The *Serie A* player of the year 2020 and 2021, she is a vital cog in the Italian squad.

BARBARA BONANSEA
BORN: 13 JUNE 1991
POSITION: MIDFIELDER/ FORWARD

A national team stalwart, she started out as a five-year-old playing boys' football, unaware that female teams existed until she was recruited by Torino at 12. Supported by her family, she made 120km round trips for training. Went on to play under Milena Bertolini at Brescia, where she was 2016 *Serie A* player of the year. A Juventus centurion, she has won multiple *Scudetto* titles since joining in 2017, and was part of the domestic treble-winning team of 2022. Nominated by her peers for the FIFA FIFPro Women's World 11 in 2020 and 2021, she is also in the Italian Hall of Fame.

time showed how much their achievement meant to the entire group.

Italy will not rest on their laurels, though, and plans to bring together the seniors and U-23s will only serve to add strength. Given they are a mostly home-based squad, last year's professionalisation of the top-flight *Serie A* and the progress of Juventus and Roma on the European club scene will be a boon too.

Formed as a national side in 1968, this is Italy's fourth appearance on the global

stage and *Le Azzurre* will be determined to put on a show once more.

WOMEN'S WORLD CUP RECORD

1991	Quarter-finalists
1995	Did not qualify
1999	Group stage (3rd)
2003	Did not qualify
2007	Did not qualify
2011	Did not qualify
2015	Did not qualify
2019	Quarter-finalists

< **89** >

G

ARGENTINA

Four years ago, *La Albiceleste* earned their first points at a FIFA Women's World Cup. Having reached back-to-back finals for a second time, this group of fighters will look to break new ground and reach the knockout phase.

COACH
GERMÁN PORTANOVA

"This is the most exciting thing I have had in my football career," declared Portanova on his appointment in July 2021. He took over from long-time manager Carlos Borrello, who was made General Coordinator of Women's Teams at the AFA. Portanova's playing career spanned clubs across South America as well as lower-league and amateur sides in Europe, but was interrupted by injury and he retired aged 36. Worked at a friend's shoe factory before returning to football as a coach. Led women's team UAI Urquiza to domestic championships and in the *Copa Libertadores*, a competition he played in with Cerro Porteño in 1998. The players cut off his pony-tail to celebrate winning bronze at the *Copa América Femenina*.

"We're in the World Cup, I can't believe it," said two-goal heroine Yamila Rodríguez after Argentina came from behind to beat Paraguay 3-1 in the third-place match at the 2022 *Copa América Femenina*.

The result guaranteed them a place at their fourth FIFA Women's World Cup finals and the singing and dancing in celebration through the post-match media zone showed just how much it meant to *La Albiceleste* to qualify for Australia & New Zealand 2023.

Their tournament had not been without its ups and downs, however.

They bounced back from an opening 4-0 loss to eventual winners Brazil by reversing

that scoreline against Peru, then dismissed Uruguay 5-0 and Venezuela 1-0, as Germán Portanova's players found their shooting boots and their stride to finish second in their group.

Hosts Colombia edged them 1-0 and Gabriela Chávez saw red in a very tight semi-final, sending them into a bronze-medal match against Paraguay.

Being a goal down at the break against their neighbours, they could have succumbed to defeat, but these are players who have battled to wear the sky-blue and white jersey and they rallied.

Firstly, Rodríguez's one-on-one finish from a route-one move pulled them level, then Florencia Bonsegundo's free kick sparked

ABOVE: Third place at the 2022 *Copa América Femenina* ensured Argentina's qualification.

scenes of joy before another similar effort from Rodríguez sealed the victory and secured South America's last direct ticket to the FIFA Women's World Cup.

Their month-long training camp and string of practice matches against male youth teams in readiness for the tournament had proved worthwhile and was a valuable level of preparation in stark contrast to the underfunding and neglect that a core of *La Albiceleste* had endured and overcome in the period leading up to France 2019.

After missing out on qualification for Canada 2015 and a dispiriting showing at the 2015 Pan American Games – due to minimal preparation – the team had no fixtures for over two years, saw their coach removed and not replaced, and became "unranked" in the eyes of FIFA due to their lack of activity.

When the Argentinian Football Association (AFA) arranged games again in August 2017, the provision for players was still so inadequate the squad released a letter of public complaint and briefly went on strike.

Relations only began to improve in April 2019 and *La Albiceleste*, still predominantly amateur but with some players on newly offered paid contracts, headed to France as under-resourced underdogs and yet competed with aplomb.

They earned their first-ever point at a senior FIFA finals in a goalless draw against 2011 winners and 2015 runners-up Japan, lost to England by a single goal – with a penalty save and goalmouth heroics from goalkeeper Vanina Correa – and fought back to level with Scotland, despite being 3-0 down with only 16 minutes remaining.

Several of the stars of that campaign, like the tireless Bonsegundo, playmaker Estefanía

VANINA CORREA
BORN: 14 AUGUST 1983
POSITION: GOALKEEPER

An enduring and eminent figure for *La Albiceleste* having made her senior debut in 2003. Experienced the 2008 Beijing Olympics, numerous continental championships – including a gold medal win in 2006 – and is the only player to have figured at all three of their FIFA Women's World Cup campaigns so far, though her only appearance before France 2019 was in the 11-0 defeat to Germany in the 2007 opening match. Known as "La Flaca", or "The Skinny One", she "retired" in late 2010 and had her twins Luna and Romeo in 2014, before then-coach Carlos Borrello persuaded her to return in 2017.

YAMILA RODRÍGUEZ
BORN: 24 JANUARY 1998
POSITION: FORWARD

A passionate, big-game player with red-hot finishing skills. Joined her beloved Boca Juniors in 2016 and had a brief spell in 2018 with Santa Teresa Badajoz in Spain. An outstanding 2022 saw her top-score at the *Copa América Femenina* and named in the tournament's best XI. Also captained Boca Juniors to yet another Argentinian championship – scoring the opener in the 2-1 title decider in front of a record crowd at the Bombonera – and the final of the *Copa Libertadores* for the first time. She has tattoos of her footballing heroes Cristiano Ronaldo and Diego Maradona on her legs.

Banini, selfless forward Mariana Larroquette and left-back Eliana Stábile, all shone in Colombia and could do again this year.

Half of Portanova's squad play in Argentina's improving domestic league, with most others in Brazil, Mexico and Spain, and so greater exposure to teams outside of CONMEBOL, such as at the SheBelieves Cup in 2021 and against Canada, Poland and Spain in the autumn of 2022, can only aid the team's development.

They have Australia & New Zealand 2023 in their sights and their ambitions are clear,

Portanova saying: "We want to win, to try to make history and qualify for the next round."

WOMEN'S WORLD CUP RECORD

1991	Did not enter
1995	Did not qualify
1999	Did not qualify
2003	Group stage (4th)
2007	Group stage (4th)
2011	Did not qualify
2015	Did not qualify
2019	Group stage (3rd)

● GERMANY

Germany conceded just two goals at France 2019, but those came in the quarter-final against rivals Sweden and were enough to end their campaign. Two-time FIFA Women's World Cup champions in the past, they are eyeing a hat-trick in 2023.

COACH
MARTINA VOSS-TECKLENBURG

Twice crowned German footballer of the year, she won a raft of domestic honours, 125 caps, four European Championships and FIFA Women's World Cup silver. As a coach with hometown club FCR Duisburg, she lifted two German Cups and the 2009 UEFA Women's Cup. Led Switzerland to a maiden FIFA Women's World Cup in 2015 and a first EURO in 2017, also winning the Cyprus Cup. Took her home nation to the quarter-finals of France 2019 and UEFA Women's EURO 2022 final. A former editor-in-chief of a German football magazine, the 55-year-old grandmother has a genuine passion for her sport, seemingly kicking every ball from the touchline.

The last time Germany added to their packed major trophy cabinet was 2016 when head coach Silvia Neid led her then-reigning European champions to Olympic gold in Rio.

Now, a new group of players has emerged and, with Neid's old team-mate Martina Voss-Tecklenburg at the helm, *Die Nationalelf* are a force to be reckoned with once again.

The proof of their resurgence came last July when they romped to the UEFA Women's EURO 2022 final, before losing in an extra-time thriller to hosts England at Wembley. It was Germany's brightest EURO showing since 2013 and

Klara Bühl, Giulia Gwinn, Marina Hegering, Lena Oberdorf and Alexandra Popp would all make the team of the tournament, with star midfielder Oberdorf named best young player.

With a stingy defence, strong and technical midfield and dangerous forward line, *Die Nationalelf* were back, but it had taken patience, resilience and self-belief to get there.

Voss-Tecklenburg had only been head coach for just over six months before the FIFA Women's World Cup 2019 and the group she led in France included 15 competition debutants. A last-eight finish offered glimpses of the promise to come, though,

ABOVE: Two-time champions Germany are resurgent and sealed qualification with a win over Türkiye.

< 92 >

as did the perfect EURO 2022 qualifying campaign that followed.

Yet 2021 was mixed, with friendly losses to France and reigning European champions the Netherlands, the first since 2000; and wins over Belgium, Australia and Norway and a goalless draw with Chile.

Flying in FIFA Women's World Cup qualification, an under-strength side left the Arnold Clark Cup in February 2022 with a draw to Spain and losses to Canada and England.

Nevertheless, the head coach insisted that Germany were not "miles away" – even if her players needed to learn to take their chances.

A strong line-up failed to do so that April, suffering a shock 3-2 loss to Serbia in FIFA Women's World Cup qualifiers. It was a first such away defeat for Germany since 1998.

Yet once her EURO 2022 squad was decided in June, the time for experimentation was over. What Voss-Tecklenburg wished for now, she said, was "courage, creativity and sometimes something crazy". The response was a thumping 7-0 win in a friendly against her former side, Switzerland.

From then on, Germany did not look back. The group she had picked for EURO 2022 included 14 from France 2019. Skipper Alexandra Popp was back after a year out injured to lead a group that were a clear blend of youth and experience.

Without conceding a goal, they adapted to the various challenges posed by Denmark, Spain, Finland and Austria before a brace from skipper Popp beat France 2-1 in the semi-final.

Losing their talismanic captain and golden boot contender in the warm-up for the final

MERLE FROHMS
BORN: 28 JANUARY 1995
POSITION: GOALKEEPER

Strong shot-stopper with super-fast reflexes, she cemented her place as No. 1 at EURO 2022 with 13 saves and four clean sheets. Won gold at the 2012 UEFA Women's U-17 Championship, making two penalty saves in the final against France. Also part of the victorious FIFA U-20 Women's World Cup 2014 squad. Signed for VfL Wolfsburg aged 16, going on to be part of their 2014 UEFA Women's Champions League winning campaign. After a spell with SC Freiburg she was ever-present for Eintracht Frankfurt in the 2020-21 *Frauen-Bundesliga* season. In 2022 she returned to the *Die Wölfinnen* as first choice between the sticks.

LINA MAGULL
BORN: 15 AUGUST 1994
POSITION: MIDFIELDER

A free-kick specialist and intelligent goalscoring midfielder with a great engine, she won multiple trophies at VfL Wolfsburg, including back-to-back UEFA Women's Champions League titles in 2013 and 2014. After impressing at SC Freiburg, she joined Bayern Munich in 2018, going on to establish herself as a key player and inspirational leader. Captained them to the *Frauen-Bundesliga* title in 2021. Wore the armband for the FIFA U-20 Women's World Cup-winning side of 2014. Made four appearances at the UEFA Women's EURO 2017, scored twice at France 2019 and three times at EURO 2022.

was a major blow and, even though Germany battled, a ninth European title was not to be.

"We'll just keep going now," said a pragmatic Voss-Tecklenburg afterwards and they did, booking their ticket to Australia & New Zealand 34 days later with a 3-0 victory over Türkiye before an almost entirely changed first XI beat Bulgaria 8-0.

A new-look Germany had kept up a historic run as one of just seven nations to reach every FIFA Women's World Cup. They will undoubtedly have prepared for these finals with vigour.

Could this be their year once more?

WOMEN'S WORLD CUP RECORD

1991	Fourth place
1995	Runners-up
1999	Quarter-finalists
2003	Winners
2007	Winners
2011	Quarter-finalists
2015	Fourth place
2019	Quarter-finalists

< 93 >

⊛ MOROCCO

Morocco made history in 2022 when they reached their first-ever Women's Africa Cup of Nations final. Now, as the first North African side to play at the FIFA Women's World Cup, a tight-knit group are ready to break new ground again.

COACH
REYNALD PEDROS

A stylish midfielder in his playing heyday who won *Ligue 1* with FC Nantes in 1995, Pedros was capped 25 times for France. He hit the ground running in his first job in women's football, a two-year spell at Olympique Lyonnais yielding back-to-back UEFA Women's Champions League titles, three domestic honours and a personal accolade as The Best FIFA Women's Coach of 2018. Parted company with Lyon by mutual consent in 2019 and took the reins at Morocco a year later. Hailed for bringing a professionalism to the national side, the 51-year-old Orléans-born coach is a driven leader with a winning mentality who sees "having fun" as a key to success.

"This is just the beginning," declared talismanic skipper Ghizlane Chebbak after the *Atlas Lionesses*' momentous quarter-final victory over Botswana in the Women's Africa Cup of Nations last July.

Hugged by singing team-mates in the midst of her player-of-the-match press conference, and with the Morocco fans' chants of "Maghrib, Maghrib" still ringing in their ears, the joy was there for all to see.

Not only were Reynald Pedros's players heading into the final four of their continental championship, they were set to do so safe in the knowledge that they had just booked a ticket to their first FIFA Women's World Cup.

Remarkably, it was the *Atlas Lionesses*' first outing at WAFCON in 22 years, the early trailblazers having fallen at the group stage in two previous appearances, in 1998 and 2000. But the signs that a new generation was ready to bring Morocco out of the shadows were there by the time 2020 dawned and they romped to a first North African Football Union Women's Tournament crown.

That summer, the Royal Moroccan Football Federation launched a four-year plan for women's football, professionalising the two-tier national league, organising an U-17 championship and introducing talent-spotting

ABOVE: Morocco are sure to make the most of their finals debut.

< 94 >

initiatives to benefit future national teams.

Of more immediate import came the appointment towards the end of the year of two-time UEFA Women's Champions League-winning coach Pedros. The Frenchman quickly proved his worth, leading a developing squad to a string of impressive results against other African nations.

A 3-0 loss away to Spain in October 2021 may have been a reality check but, in the year before the opening WAFCON match, it would be their only defeat in 11 under the former Lyon boss.

The squad that Pedros had settled on for WAFCON was global in reach but cohesive in spirit. Moroccan top-flight AS FAR professionals such as Chebbak, Fatima Tagnaout, Sanaa Mssoudy and Zineb Redouani were in the mix, as were Europe-based youngsters Nesryne El Chad, Samya Hassani and Sabah Seghir, and national-team veterans Salma Amani and Elodie Nakkach. Former England youth striker Rosella Ayane and Yasmin Mrabet, a UEFA Women's U-19 Championship winner with Spain in 2018, were included in the group too.

All would step up, the victories continuing to come in the continental showpiece as Morocco powered their way into the knockouts – the first Arab nation to achieve that feat.

Thriving on the pressure as hosts and relishing the support of record crowds, Morocco would follow up their last-eight joy with a shock semi-final win over 11-time champions Nigeria in front of 45,562 cheering fans.

Nigeria took the lead, despite having a player red-carded, and never gave up, even after Mssoudy's equaliser and another dismissal. But urged on amid a riot of noise, Morocco would emerge victorious, Ayane scoring

GHIZLANE CHEBBAK
BORN: 22 AUGUST 1990
POSITION: MIDFIELDER

A dead-ball specialist and visionary playmaker who debuted for her country in 2007, following in the footsteps of her late father, Larbi. A multiple Moroccan Championship and Throne Cup winner with Rabat-based club AS FAR, she has also been crowned her country's player of the year a record five times. Joint top scorer in the Women's Africa Cup of Nations, the *Atlas Lionesses'* classy captain led by example, finishing as the tournament's best player. Shortlisted for the prestigious CAF Women's Player of the Year award in 2022, this Casablanca native is a widely respected figure in African football.

ROSELLA AYANE
BORN: 16 MARCH 1996
POSITION: FORWARD

This former England youth player switched to represent Morocco, the birthplace of her father, in 2021. In just over a year, she had written her name into the nation's history books after scoring the penalty that took Morocco into the Women's Africa Cup of Nations final, going on to score in the final too. A skilful, hardworking team player with bags of experience in the English WSL, the "Roadrunner" made her senior debut at Chelsea aged 17. She impressed at Cypriot top-flight club Apollon Ladies in 2017, scoring 19 goals in 19 games. Joined Tottenham Hotspur in 2019, becoming a key player for the north London side.

the winning spot kick in a penalty shoot-out to send her team through.

Pedros hailed the supporters at full time and they came out in their thousands again in the final, but South Africa would have the edge.

Even so, it had been a colossal achievement. The future certainly looks bright for Morocco and, while a tough challenge awaits all those players who don the red and green at this World Cup, they can be sure that the hearts and minds of an expectant North Africa will go with them.

WOMEN'S WORLD CUP RECORD

This will be a first appearance at the showpiece finals for the *Atlas Lionesses*, who qualified after finishing as one of the top four sides in the Women's Africa Cup of Nations in July 2022.

● COLOMBIA

South America's second-ranked side are aiming to do better than ever when they return to the FIFA Women's World Cup. *Las Cafeteras* have surprised sides on the big stage before and have the ingredients to do it again this year.

COACH
NELSON ABADÍA

The 67-year-old Cali-based coach has experience of working with men's teams in the lower divisions in Colombia and with one of Panama's biggest and most successful clubs, Tauro FC. He was Fabian Taborda's right-hand man during the FIFA Women's World Cup 2015 as well as their 2014 *Copa América Femenina* and 2015 Pan American Games silver-medal campaigns. He then managed the América de Cali women's team briefly in 2016 before taking charge of *Las Cafeteras* in September 2017. Led them to their first-ever major title at the 2019 Pan American Games and has used his platform to advocate for Dimayor, the organisers of Colombia's women's professional *Liga Femenina*, to provide a better competition for his home-based players.

Colombia coach Nelson Abadía was full of praise for his team's performance in the final of the 2022 *Copa América Femenina* against Brazil, proudly describing the players as "extraordinary" and "brilliant".

They actually lost the game 1-0, having conceded a first-half penalty after Manuela Vanegas's foul on Debinha, but *Las Cafeteras* had responded with such character and verve, created several chances and, most pleasingly for Abadía, displayed their footballing identity.

The fans appreciated the efforts of the first-time hosts too, filling the stands with a sea of yellow and creating a carnival atmosphere in and around the stadiums, culminating in the sold-out final, played at Estadio Alfonso López in Bucaramanga.

Before the ultimate disappointment of missing out on the continental crown, their 1-0 semi-final win over Argentina had ensured they were the first South American side to bag a spot at the FIFA Women's World Cup 2023 and, with the same result, they booked a place in the Paris 2024 Olympic Games too.

Securing qualification ended an eight-year absence for Colombia at the FIFA Women's World Cup – they last appeared in 2015, where they shocked France 2-0 in the group stage and made it to the round of 16 before losing by the same scoreline to

ABOVE: Colombia's feel-good factor sees them return for a third finals appearance.

< 96 >

eventual champions, the USA. It also marked a return to the Olympics after missing out on the Tokyo Games.

That crucial last-four *Copa América* victory against Argentina came courtesy of teenage sensation Linda Caicedo's lone strike in the second half after forward Mayra Ramírez had rattled the bar in the first.

Aged only 17 at the time, the lithe young forward, who loves to dart in from the left, was named player of the tournament and often proved the difference for *Las Cafeteras* on their unbeaten charge to the final.

She was not alone, though. Several of the experienced characters within Abadía's fairly settled 4-2-3-1 line-up produced the goods in the run to their third *Copa América Femenina* final too.

Las Cafeteras' all-time leading goalscorer Catalina Usme, often in the No. 10 role, skipper Daniela Montoya in the centre of the park, and youngster Caicedo were included in the "ideal" team of the tournament.

"We're so happy to be going to the Olympics and the World Cup," enthused goalkeeper Catalina Perez. "And we don't just want to go; we want to do better than any Colombia team has done before."

It has not been an easy road for Colombia since their last appearance on the world stage. The team went 400 days without a game after Rio. In 2019, a group of players went public with complaints that they were being treated like "second-class citizens" by their association. Their grievances ranged from missing payments to poor facilities, no full-time coach and a lack of training.

But with support from players' unions, government and other bodies, the situation has

CATALINA USME
BORN: 25 DECEMBER 1989
POSITION: MIDFIELDER/ FORWARD

Left-footed playmaker and sometime striker, she is *Las Cafeteras*' all-time top scorer. Her numerous and impressive goal-grabbing achievements include leading the 2018 *Copa América Femenina* with nine in seven games, bagging the all-time highest goal tally in the continental club competition, the *Copa Libertadores* and, now with América de Cali, the first to reach 50 goals in Colombia's professional *Liga Femenina*. She netted in the 2-0 shock win over France at the FIFA Women's World Cup 2015 and scored two free kicks in a 2-2 draw with USA at the Rio Olympics in 2016.

LINDA CAICEDO
BORN: 22 FEBRUARY 2005
POSITION: FORWARD

Known as "the Colombian Neymar" for her speed, dribbling skills and finishing ability. Combining those qualities with an on-field maturity that belies her age, she is one of the game's hottest young talents. Joined América de Cali and dribbled home a stunning solo goal on her *Liga Femenina* debut, aged 14. Went on to win the league with América and then city rivals Deportivo Cali. In 2022, she played in and scored at three major tournaments, being named best player at the *Copa América Femenina*, netting twice at the FIFA U-20 Women's World Cup and claiming the Silver Ball and Bronze Boot in the U-17 edition.

improved and *Las Cafeteras*' programme appears to be thriving.

In 2019, the senior side claimed their first major silverware, lifting the Pan American Games trophy in Lima.

Then, in the months following the 2022 *Copa América Femenina*, the U-20s progressed to the quarter-finals of their FIFA Women's World Cup, and the U-17s, captained by Caicedo, made history by winning through to Colombia's first-ever global final, where they lost to defending champions Spain by

a single goal. Could *Las Cafeteras* make 2023 another year to savour?

WOMEN'S WORLD CUP RECORD

1991	Did not enter
1995	Did not enter
1999	Did not qualify
2003	Did not qualify
2007	Did not qualify
2011	Group stage (4th)
2015	Round of 16
2019	Did not qualify

GROUP H

KOREA REPUBLIC

The *Taeguk Ladies* skirted so close to winning their first-ever major senior trophy at the AFC Women's Asian Cup in 2022. Their ambition is to compete with and beat the best. What better place to continue that mission than at Australia & New Zealand 2023?

COACH
COLIN BELL

Former professional who left Leicester City to play in Germany in 1982. Worked there for over two decades in a variety of head- and assistant-coaching, academy and scouting roles at men's clubs, including at 1. FSV Mainz 05 during Jürgen Klopp's tenure. Has coached SC 07 Bad Neuenahr, SC Sand and Norwegian club Avaldsnes in the women's game. Guided 1. FFC Frankfurt to UEFA Women's Champions League victory in 2015 and managed Republic of Ireland Women from 2017 to 2019. Bell started learning Korean as soon as he accepted the Korea Republic job in October 2019.

When Ji So-yun arrived at WK League side Suwon FC from Chelsea in May 2022, after eight years as one of the English Women's Super League's most successful foreign imports, the media interest was muted compared to the one she had just left behind.

This was an iconic, world-class midfielder about to play her first senior domestic season in her home country, so it neatly highlighted the work the women's game still has to do to reach the mainstream in Korea Republic.

A 2021 reality TV show featuring female celebrities learning to play football called "Kick a Goal" caused an explosion of interest and participation. Yet success for the women's national team – which will inspire its own legacy – is what role models like Ji and the Korea FA are striving towards.

The FIFA Women's World Cup 2015 had delighted Korean football fans and hinted at exciting times ahead when the *Taeguk Ladies* came from behind to beat Spain and reach the knockout phase.

However, their campaign four years later ended in a deflating exit after three group-stage defeats, against the hosts France, Nigeria and Norway. Further disappointment followed in April 2021 when a goal in extra time meant China PR edged them 4-3 in a two-legged play-off for the

ABOVE: Korea Republic's ambitions are clear – they want to compete with the best.

< 98 >

delayed 2020 Tokyo Olympics.

Positive foundations had been laid 18 months earlier, though, with the appointment of Englishman Colin Bell as head coach, the first foreigner to take the role.

Now, an athletically improving and experienced squad is becoming more tactically versatile and growing in belief too, with the gains made evident in their brilliant run to the final of the AFC Women's Asian Cup in India.

There were comfortable 3-0 and 2-0 successes over a COVID-19-weakened Vietnam and Myanmar, respectively. Then came a mood-boosting 1-1 draw against Japan thanks to Seo Ji-youn's scrappy equaliser five minutes from time.

That set up a daunting quarter-final versus the highest-ranked team, Australia. An energetic encounter saw both sides miss chances until, three minutes from time and from 25 yards out, Ji So-yun fired in the tournament's top-ranked goal from open play to secure the 1-0 win and a place at Australia & New Zealand 2023.

The result against the *Matildas* was considered a shock, but not to Bell and his focused players – Korea Republic are the highest-ranked Asian nation never to have won the continental title.

In the semi-final, they dismissed Philippines 2-0 through Cho So-hyun and Son Hwa-yeon's first-half goals to move one step closer to the prize and exorcise the ghosts of four previous semi-final losses.

Beginning confidently in the heat of the final in Navi Mumbai against old foes China PR, they were 2-0 to the good after striker Choe Yu-ri converted Lee Geum-min's cross and Ji So-yun buried her penalty following a VAR review that spotted Yao Lingwei's handball.

CHO SO-HYUN
BORN: 24 JUNE 1988
POSITION: MIDFIELDER

Dynamic, experienced, central midfielder and team captain. Clinched four WK League titles with Incheon Hyundai Steel Red Angels and won the 2016 Empress's Cup while on loan to INAC Kobe Leonessa in Japan. Joined Avaldsnes in 2018, the first South Korean woman to sign for a Norwegian club. Spent 2019 to 2021 with West Ham United in the English WSL. Made a loan move to Tottenham Hotspur permanent in July 2021. Headed the equaliser in a comeback win against Spain in 2015, which carried the *Taeguk Ladies* to the knockout stages of the FIFA Women's World Cup for the first time.

They were facing the tournament's comeback queens, however, and China PR pegged them back to 2-2. Then, seconds after Korea Republic failed to score in stoppage time from close range at one end, in a heartbreaking climax, the Chinese raced forward and snatched the winner.

Results since, including a goalless friendly draw with Olympic champions Canada, suggest that the *Taeguk Ladies* continue to look to the future with growing confidence. Bell has tremendous confidence in his talented squad and believes they

JI SO-YUN
BORN: 21 FEBRUARY 1991
POSITION: MIDFIELDER

Korea Republic's youngest-ever player and scorer – aged 15 in 2006 – and the nation's all-time top scorer, overtaking men's football legend Cha Bum-kun. Ebullient personality and a special type of box-to-box playmaker. So often provides a moment of quality or spectacular goal on the biggest occasions. Seven-time winner of KFA player of the year and the first South Korean in the English WSL following her move from Japan's title-winning INAC Kobe Leonessa to Chelsea. Made the PFA WSL Team of the Year five times. Instrumental in 11 major trophy successes with Chelsea across eight seasons.

are capable of beating any team. Now would be a fine time to fulfil that promise.

WOMEN'S WORLD CUP RECORD

1991	Did not qualify
1995	Did not qualify
1999	Did not qualify
2003	Group stage (4th)
2007	Did not qualify
2011	Did not qualify
2015	Round of 16
2019	Group stage (4th)

FIFA WOMEN'S WORLD CUP SUPERSTARS

❋

Since 1991, some of the greatest names in women's football have graced this world stage. These finals will be a showcase for many more. From established global superstars like the USA's Alex Morgan and Debinha of Brazil, to class acts in their prime such as Nigeria's Asisat Oshoala and Japan's Saki Kumagai, and outrageously talented youngsters who play beyond their years like Germany's Lena Oberdorf, all can light up this tournament.

KOSOVARE ASLLANI

Kosovare Asllani brings grace, graft, dead-ball accuracy and defence-splitting passes to a Sweden side that has seen medal successes in recent major tournaments.

One of the standout players in the *Blågult* team that finished third at the FIFA Women's World Cup 2019 and won silver at the last two Olympic Games. Asllani was their top scorer with three in France, including a goal in the 2-1 bronze-medal triumph over England.

Born in Kristianstad after her parents moved to Sweden in 1988, she grew up playing at Vimmerby IF where, in 2018, she was honoured with an eponymous football facility, Asllani Court.

"Kosse"'s national-team debut came aged 19 in 2008 and, though she played at the 2009 UEFA Women's EURO, she was devastated to miss out on the FIFA Women's World Cup 2011. Bouncing back, she featured at the London 2012 Olympics and has worn the No. 9 at every major tournament since.

Her incisive distribution and technical skills are a joy to watch in her playmaker role for Sweden, though her shrewd sense of positioning and highly effective defensive work are often overlooked. In fact, her pressing and tenacity are integral to how Peter Gerhardsson's team play – she was 2017 Swedish player of the year in his first season in charge.

At domestic level, Asllani is still sometimes deployed as a striker, utilising her sharp instincts in the box. Her adventurous club career has taken in six countries so far, including several spells in her native Sweden with Linköpings FC, the USA with Chicago Red Stars and Paris Saint-Germain in France.

In 2016, she ventured to Manchester City and helped them win their only English Women's Super League title to date plus two cups, despite being played out wide for most of her time there.

Never one to shy away from pressure or expectation, she was the first "Galáctica" when signing for CD Tacón in 2019 – the side that turned into Real Madrid the following season – and scored the first-ever goal, brace and hat-trick for *Las Blancas*. In the summer of 2022, she headed to Italy and is thriving in the *rossonero* of AC Milan.

Asllani is an exemplar for girls of foreign origin in Sweden. She has a tattoo of the black double-headed eagle of Albania on her ankle and is outspoken on issues she cares about.

FACTS AND FIGURES

BORN: 29 JULY 1989
POSITION: MIDFIELDER/ FORWARD
CLUBS: LINKÖPINGS FC (SWE), CHICAGO RED STARS (USA), KRISTIANSTADS DFF (SWE), PARIS SAINT-GERMAIN (FRA), MANCHESTER CITY (ENG), CD TACÓN/REAL MADRID (ESP), AC MILAN (ITA)
CAPS/GOALS: 169/44

< 102 >

LUCY BRONZE

Lucy Bronze's haul of winners' medals and host of major individual awards as a full-back demonstrate just how special an athlete, competitor and inspirational figure she has become.

FACTS AND FIGURES

BORN: 28 OCTOBER 1991
POSITION: DEFENDER
CLUBS: SUNDERLAND (ENG), EVERTON (ENG), LIVERPOOL (ENG), MANCHESTER CITY (ENG), OLYMPIQUE LYONNAIS (FRA), FC BARCELONA (ESP)
CAPS/GOALS: 100/11

Lucy Bronze is widely regarded as the finest right-back in the women's game. Her all-action style combines effective forays forward with dedicated, front-foot defending. Her driving runs with the ball can spur on team-mates, as does her infectious desire to win. And her middle name, "Tough", speaks volumes about her reliability.

She may revel in thwarting talented forwards but it was the screamer she scored against Norway at the FIFA Women's World Cup 2015 that made her a household name. England won bronze at the tournament and Bronze was named in the all-star squad.

In a breakthrough 2009, she collected the player of the match award in the FA Cup final for second-tier Sunderland, won the UEFA Women's U-19 Championship with England and became the first-ever British NCAA College Cup champion, with the University of North Carolina.

Her resilience was tested by four knee surgeries before the age of 18, leading to extended time on the sidelines – she still plays with residual pain, despite a fifth operation in 2021 – but with hard work and patience there was better to come.

Following back-to-back Women's Super League titles with Liverpool, another league win plus cup victories with Manchester City and England's run to the 2017 UEFA Women's EURO semi-finals, she took her ambition to all-conquering Olympique Lyonnais.

While in France, Bronze secured three UEFA Women's Champions League-winning medals, three French domestic titles and three cup successes.

Further accolades arrived including BBC Women's Footballer of the Year in 2018 and 2020, the silver ball for second-best player at FIFA Women's World Cup 2019 and the UEFA Women's Player of the Year award soon after. *Ballon d'Or féminin* nominations followed and then, in 2020, FIFA's highest individual honour too. Bronze's influence was huge as the Lionesses grasped European glory in 2022 and she earned her 100th cap last October.

> **"I think sometimes we take her performances for granted because she's Lucy Bronze and she's one of the best players in the world. But to keep doing that game in game out, I think she's incredible."**
>
> JILL SCOTT, *former England midfielder*

< 103 >

KADEISHA BUCHANAN

From being hailed as the best young player of the FIFA Women's World Cup 2015, Kadeisha Buchanan's career has gone from strength to strength. She is one of Canada's most dependable stars.

FACTS AND FIGURES

BORN: 5 NOVEMBER 1995
POSITION: DEFENDER
CLUBS: OLYMPIQUE LYONNAIS (FRA), CHELSEA (ENG)
CAPS/GOALS: 128/4

The youngest of seven sisters, Kadeisha "Keisha" Buchanan was born into what she describes as an "all-round sporting family" and recalls watching the English Premier League every weekend with her Manchester United-supporting dad.

She was a professional footballer herself by 2017, joining Olympique Lyonnais straight from college at the same time as USA superstar Alex Morgan.

Buchanan enjoyed an illustrious career with OL. The first Canadian to win the UEFA Women's Champions League, she would lift the trophy five times, while also claiming three French cups and five league titles.

Yet this Ontario native did not rest on her laurels, opting in 2022 to join Chelsea in England's Women's Super League.

In addition to her fine positional awareness, speed and skill on the ball, a readiness to go beyond her comfort zone is another of her impressive traits.

A feted college player in the USA, she juggled a criminology degree with star turns for West Virginia University and the Canadian national set-up in her late teens, winning multiple personal honours for both.

Named Canada's best U-20 player two years running, in the wake of Canada's quarter-final berth at the FIFA U-20 Women's World Cup 2014 on home soil, she made the all-star squad.

By the end of 2015, the defender had the world at her feet. Crowned the young player of that year's FIFA Women's World Cup in Canada, she made the FIFA FIFPRO Women's World 11, was nominated for the *Ballon d'Or féminin* and won the first of her three Canadian player of the year gongs.

That she ended legendary striker Christine Sinclair's 11-year dominance of the award seemed ironic given that after shaking hands with "Sinc" on their first-ever meeting, Buchanan had vowed never to wash hers again.

Together, though, they would help Canada capture Olympic bronze in 2016 and triumph with gold in 2021. Now, at 27 and with over a century of caps, the defender sits alongside Sinclair as one of Canada's leaders.

She is a big-game player too and, having been ever-present at the last two finals, will look to make an impact as Canada chase silverware at Australia & New Zealand 2023.

"She has world-class qualities that any country would be proud to have and she is a highly valued member of the squad both on and off the pitch."

BEV PRIESTMAN, *Canada head coach*

< 104 >

DEBINHA

A humble, diminutive and determined character with bags of speed and agility, she has claimed multiple individual awards and team titles in the National Women's Soccer League.

Debinha is desperate to secure success to honour the greats that have paved the way for the current *Seleção*. Players like Cristiane, Formiga and Marta are inspirational female icons but, with more than a century of caps and over 50 goals to her name, Debinha has blossomed into the newest superstar in yellow and green.

A regular in the national team since Rio 2016, the 31-year-old has established herself as a driving force in Pia Sundhage's side and the most prolific scorer since the Swede took the helm in 2019.

As a little girl in Minas Gerais, Debinha's football flame was ignited by the collective excitement of cheering on the men's *Seleção* and the joy of playing with a ball, gifted by her PE teacher, in the local square with her two sisters and neighbourhood friends.

Football was her means to escape, both figuratively and literally. Aged 15, she bravely moved away from her beloved family and signed for the pioneering, star-studded Saad side several hundred miles away.

It was the beginning of a club football journey that would take her from Brazil, via Norway and China PR, to the USA.

Since joining the NWSL in January 2017, she has helped North Carolina Courage to three Shields and two Championships as one of the league's most consistent and admired performers.

In the 2022 NWSL Challenge Cup, she went on a five-game goalscoring run and was named MVP for the second successive year, later that season being included in the league's Best XI First Team too.

She may only be 5'2" (157cm) but her work rate, awareness, strength, balance and finishing make her one of the best in the world on her day.

Despite representing Brazil at two Olympic Games and twice winning gold at the *Copa América Femenina*, a serious knee injury before Canada 2015 meant Debinha had to wait till France 2019 to make her FIFA Women's World Cup debut. She played every minute and it was "a dream come true".

Her array of tattoos include ones acknowledging her family and her resilience, but her favourite serves as both inspiration and perhaps a warning to opponents: "When I think I've reached my limit, I find that I have the strength to go beyond..."

"She's unselfish and brings out the best in other performers. She's tricky, crafty, sly, has great endurance and scores goals – that's some combination."

PIA SUNDHAGE, *Brazil head coach*

FACTS AND FIGURES

BORN: 20 OCTOBER 1991
POSITION: MIDFIELDER/ FORWARD
CLUBS: SAAD ESPORTE CLUBE (BRA), PORTUGUESA (BRA), FOZ CATARATAS (BRA), CENTRO OLÍMPICO (BRA), AVALDSNES (NOR), SÃO JOSÉ (LOAN, BRA), DALIAN QUANJIAN (CHN), NORTH CAROLINA COURAGE (USA), KANSAS CITY CURRENT (USA)
CAPS/GOALS: 132/57

< 105 >

PERNILLE HARDER

Twice named the best player in Europe, Denmark skipper Pernille Harder boasts a reputation as one of the continent's most energetic, intelligent and creative attackers.

Pernille Harder was just ten years old when she first dreamt of being a professional footballer. By the age of 27, she had become the world's most expensive signing.

Since making that headline-grabbing move to Chelsea for a reported £250,000 in 2020, Harder has won a string of domestic titles and helped the *Blues* clinch their maiden, and her third, UEFA Women's Champions League silver.

She also became the first to claim two UEFA Women's Player of the Year awards, making the top three in The Best FIFA Women's Player nominations and a place in the FIFA FIFPRO Women's World 11 to boot.

In September 2021, Denmark's No. 10 wrote her name into the history books when she overtook Merete Pedersen's record of 65 to become her country's all-time leading scorer, male or female.

There is more to Harder's talent than killer goals, though. Her work rate is consistently high and, as technical observers at last summer's UEFA Women's EURO noted, she can link attacks, find space, hold up the ball, embark on solo runs and make a telling pass.

Hers is a talent honed from a young age, Harder having followed her older sister Louise into football, playing alongside boys until the age of 11, before going on to join Team Viborg at 14.

In 2010 she switched to another Danish top-flight side, Skovbakken, where she would terrorise defences alongside fellow future national-team legend Nadia Nadim.

By then, Harder had already played in the FIFA U-17 Women's World Cup with Denmark aged 15 and had bagged a hat-trick on her senior debut at 16.

She went on to lay down markers of her talent at consecutive EUROs, playing her part as Denmark reached the semis in 2013 and captaining her side to silver in 2017.

A consistent performer at club level, she has top-scored in the *Damallsvenskan* with Linköpings FC as well as in the *Frauen-Bundesliga* and UEFA Women's Champions League with Wolfsburg, where she enjoyed four double-winning seasons.

Off the pitch, Harder and her long-time partner, Chelsea skipper and Sweden international Magdalena Eriksson, are part of the Common Goal Play Proud initiative to create safe sporting spaces for LGBTQ+ youth worldwide.

FACTS AND FIGURES

BORN: 15 NOVEMBER 1992
POSITION: FORWARD
CLUBS: TEAM VIBORG (DEN), IK SKOVBAKKEN (DEN), LINKÖPINGS FC (SWE), VFL WOLFSBURG (GER), CHELSEA (ENG)
CAPS/GOALS: 140/70

"Her standards day-in, day-out should be what every young person should look up to. She takes responsibility, she's accountable, she's there when it really matters. She is an outstanding player and person."

EMMA HAYES, *Chelsea manager*

< 106 >

ADA HEGERBERG

With technical acumen and plenty of goals, Hegerberg is a winner. She is the UEFA Women's Champions League all-time top scorer and only the second woman to be crowned Norway's best footballer.

Ada Hegerberg wrote her name into football folklore on a remarkable night in Turin in May 2022 as Lyon overwhelmed Barcelona 3-1 to win an eighth UEFA Women's Champions League crown.

In heading home *Les Lyonnaises'* second goal, the Norwegian became one of just two players to score in four European finals – the first being men's great, Alfredo Di Stefano.

It was not the first time this instinctive striker had caused a stir. Aged 16, she hit the headlines in Norway after scoring a seven-minute hat-trick for Kolbotn in the *Toppserien*.

UEFA's best player in 2016, two years later she became the first to win the *Ballon d'Or féminin* and, in 2019, claimed the mantle of all-time top UEFA Women's Champions League scorer.

Signing off the 2021-22 season with a sixth European and seventh league title with Lyon was special, though. Hegerberg had only returned from an anterior cruciate ligament injury in October.

With the support of her parents, brother and fellow footballing professionals, sister Andrine and husband Thomas Rogne, she had held on to her self-belief throughout her long recuperation.

As her goals in the league campaign and UEFA Women's Champions League group stage, quarter-final, semi-final and final showed, she had certainly lost none of the attributes that make her the player she is.

How did she get so good? An ambitious but likeable character with a firm team ethic, Hegerberg is an ardent believer in the benefits of hard work, discipline and hours of repetition and practice.

Hegerberg missed France 2019, still in the midst of a self-imposed exile from the national team after calling for improvements and respect for the women's game in her homeland.

She returned in April 2022, believing the time was right and having had positive discussions with new Norwegian FA President Lise Klaveness.

In typical fashion, the talismanic forward marked her first game back for Norway, in the snow against Kosovo, with a hat-trick.

Even Hegerberg could do little about a dismal 2022 UEFA Women's EURO campaign but, looking to the future, expect her to do all she can to get Norway back on the international map.

"Ada has a physical and mental strength above the norm. She is on her way to becoming the best player in the world."

JEAN-MICHEL AULAS, *Lyon President*

FACTS AND FIGURES

BORN: 10 JULY 1995
POSITION: FORWARD
CLUBS: KOLBOTN (NOR), STABÆK (NOR), 1.FFC TURBINE POTSDAM (GER), OLYMPIQUE LYONNAIS (FRA)
CAPS/GOALS: 74/42

< 107 >

SAM KERR

Australia's leading scorer and inspirational captain, Sam Kerr is a global superstar who has hit the scoring heights on three continents. She is renowned for her trademark back-flip celebration.

FACTS AND FIGURES

BORN: 10 SEPTEMBER 1993
POSITION: FORWARD
CLUBS: PERTH GLORY (AUS), SYDNEY FC (AUS), WESTERN NEW YORK FLASH (USA), SKY BLUE FC (USA), CHICAGO RED STARS (USA), CHELSEA (ENG)
CAPS/GOALS: 116/61

There were sharp intakes of breath all round in the English game in 2019 when the news came through that Chelsea had captured the signature of *Matildas* captain Sam Kerr.

The all-time leading scorer in Australia's W-League and the USA's National Women's Soccer League, Kerr had scored five goals at that year's FIFA Women's World Cup.

By the close of 2019, the Perth-born forward had also been named the NWSL's Most Valuable Player for an unprecedented second time and Golden Boot for a record third consecutive season.

Since then, Kerr has kicked on to another level, winning a raft of personal honours and team titles.

With Chelsea, the lightning fast, fearless and selfless forward has forged successful attacking partnerships with England's Fran Kirby and Denmark's Pernille Harder, triumphing in the league and both domestic cup competitions.

Kerr has added the Women's Super League to her Golden Boot tally and, in 2022, she ranked second in The Best FIFA Women's Player of the Year awards and third in the *Ballon d'Or féminin* for a second successive season.

Appointed Australia skipper in 2019 ahead of her third FIFA Women's World Cup, she has also cemented her reputation as an icon in green and gold.

In 2021, she captained the *Matildas* to a historic fourth place at the Tokyo Olympics, scoring a crucial extra-time winner against Team GB, later earning her 100th cap.

In India last year at her fourth AFC Women's Asian Cup, she overtook Tim Cahill's record of 50 to become her country's all-time top goalscorer. It was a moment to relish for this Australian with proud Indian heritage.

All were remarkable achievements too, considering she was solely invested in Australian rules football until the age of 12 when she had to stop playing alongside boys.

A latecomer to soccer, Kerr still debuted for the *Matildas* at 15. Yet she has had to learn her trade and dig deep to overcome a career-threatening knee injury in her early 20s.

Now a children's author with one million followers on Instagram, she remains grounded nevertheless and is regarded within football circles as a humble, easy-going team player and role model.

"Sam's grown the game huge in Australia, not only for females but for young boys and men as well. Her stepping on to the world stage and performing at that level has definitely pushed the game even further to where it is now."

CAITLIN FOORD, *Australia forward*

< 108 >

SAKI KUMAGAI

Few players have an array of medals and memories from major finals comparable to the collection amassed by 2019 AFC Women's Player of the Year, Saki Kumagai.

Saki Kumagai scored the decisive fourth penalty that clinched Japan's historic FIFA Women's World Cup 2011 crown. Cool as you like, her shoot-out spot kick rose unopposed into the top-left corner to seal victory against the USA.

At only 20 years old, she was a rookie in the team but it pushed her name to the fore. Incredibly, she says she enjoyed the moment and did not feel nerves.

An air of serenity has always been a characteristic of the Hokkaido native's style. Adept in aerial battles and one-on-one defensive duels, she is a supreme reader of the game and comfortable in possession.

Kumagai attributes these skills to growing up playing in boys' football until the age of 15 – they were faster than her, which promoted speed of thought and planning ahead. Her savvy passing can trigger quick transitions from defence to attack.

Alongside a successful youth career for school and country, she made her senior international debut in 2008, aged 17, and won the Nadeshiko League in her first season with Urawa Reds.

When she moved to the *Frauen-Bundesliga* with 1. FFC Frankfurt, after Germany 2011, it was the start of a European odyssey unrivalled by any other player from Asia.

Kumagai further impressed as Japan earned silver at the London 2012 Olympic Games and signed for Olympique Lyonnais in June 2013, going on to excel in a defensive midfield role for the emerging European women's football superpower.

Across eight seasons in France, she scored 42 goals in 226 appearances and amassed an impressive 19 trophies, including five UEFA Women's Champions League titles, reprising her role as shoot-out heroine in the 2016 final against VfL Wolfsburg. She also banged in a long-range beauty against the same opposition in the 2020 decider to become the first Asian player to score in the prestige fixture. In 2021, she returned to Germany with Bayern Munich.

Japan's defensive lynchpin and leader, Kumagai has played over 130 times for her country – also winning silver at Canada 2015 and gold at both the 2010 Asian Games and 2018 AFC Women's Asian Cup – and has been captain since 2017.

"She is an exceptional player. She has a huge influence mentally and also tactically. She is one of the best players I have ever coached."

GÉRARD PRÊCHEUR, *former Lyon coach*

FACTS AND FIGURES

BORN: 17 OCTOBER 1990
POSITION: DEFENDER/ MIDFIELDER
CLUBS: URAWA RED DIAMONDS LADIES (JPN), 1.FFC FRANKFURT (GER), OLYMPIQUE LYONNAIS (FRA), BAYERN MUNICH (GER)
CAPS/GOALS: 131/2

<109>

VIVIANNE MIEDEMA

Ice-cool striker Vivianne Miedema is one of football's big-game players, firing in the goals for club and country when it matters. She is the Netherlands' all-time top scorer.

FACTS AND FIGURES

BORN: 15 JULY 1996
POSITION: FORWARD
CLUBS: SC HEERENVEEN (NED), BAYERN MUNICH (GER), ARSENAL (ENG)
CAPS/GOALS: 115/95

Vivianne Miedema was 16 when she bagged a record eight goals in one UEFA Women's U-17 Championship qualifier and just 18 when she top-scored with six, including the winner in the final against Spain, to help secure the European title for the U-19s.

Her early achievements in a senior shirt were phenomenal too. A mere 17-year-old when she hit a remarkable 16-minute hat-trick on only her second outing, a year later her three play-off goals secured a historic first FIFA Women's World Cup berth.

Miedema's world-class reputation was cemented in the home UEFA Women's EURO of 2017, her big-game mentality shining through in the final as her brace against Denmark helped secure her side's first major title.

A runner-up at France 2019, this two-footed marvel also became the *Oranje Leeuwinnen*'s leading scorer at the age of just 22, while her ten goals at the Olympics in 2021 was the most scored by any Dutch player in any major tournament, men's or women's.

Growing up watching her striker dad play, Miedema perfected her own technique by putting little brother Lars in goal while she pinged in shots and tried not to hit him.

She honed her talent alongside boys at hometown clubs HZVV and then VV de Weide before signing her first professional women's contract with SC Heerenveen aged 14 and twice top-scoring in the BeNe League.

Today, this tall and skilful striker is a role model not just in her homeland, but in England too. After winning two *Frauen-Bundesliga* titles with Bayern Munich, she switched to English club Arsenal, where she has achieved legendary status.

Wearing the No. 11 shirt of her childhood hero, Robin van Persie, she has racked up over a century of goals for the Gunners and is also the Women's Super League all-time top scorer.

A complete team player who is comfortable up top or as a playmaking No. 10, Miedema has twice made the FIFA FIFPRO Women's World 11 and was BBC Women's Footballer of the Year in 2021.

Her 2022-23 season ended early with an ACL injury last December so fans across the world will eye her recovery keenly ahead of these global finals.

> **"She is very intelligent, has high demands like any excellent player, she views the game from her lens. I always learn new things when I speak to Viv and she has very clear ideas but is also open to change and listening."**
>
> JONAS EIDEVALL, *Arsenal head coach*

< 110 >

ALEX MORGAN

With her lethal left foot and intelligent movement, Alex Morgan is one of the world's best finishers. In three FIFA Women's World Cups, the USA's No. 13 has bagged nine goals.

Alex Morgan is no stranger to success, boasting winners' medals in the UEFA Women's Champions League and Olympics, plus one U-20 and two senior FIFA Women's World Cups.

Crowned US Soccer and Concacaf player of the year multiple times, she has also been named in several Concacaf Best XI and FIFA FIFPRO Women's World 11 teams.

At the FIFA Women's World Cup 2019 she scored five in one match to equal USA legend Michelle Akers' long-standing record, later coming second in The Best FIFA Women's Player award and third in that year's *Ballon d'Or féminin*.

She has just turned 34 but, having already kicked on after giving birth to her daughter Charlie in May 2020 by winning Olympic bronze, she has proven her mettle once again.

During a stellar 2022, this fearless fox-in-the-box and penalty queen bagged 15 goals in 17 league games to claim the National Women's Soccer League Golden Boot.

In USA colours, she took best player honours at the Concacaf W Championship, her clinical penalty from the spot in the final against Canada helping her country win gold for a third time on the bounce.

Remarkably, the USA's iconic No. 13 only started out in club football aged 14 and was still at college in her native California when she made her international debut in 2010.

The youngest player on her country's roster at Germany 2011, she made her mark as the first from the USA to get a goal and assist in a FIFA Women's World Cup final.

Dubbed "Baby Horse" for her running style in those early days, this fearless forward has matured into a thoroughbred, contributing crucial goals and memorable moments for club and country.

A successful children's author with an Instagram following of 9.7 million, Morgan is also one of the most recognised names in world football.

She uses that fame to great effect and has worked with UNICEF as a Global Athlete Ambassador and is part of the Common Goal movement.

A passionate advocate for equal pay and players' rights, this veteran is a leader for the USA both on and off the pitch.

"Alex is a USWNT legend. She is an incredible person first and foremost, an incredible leader and very good player, she has helped build this programme and win championships."

VLATKO ANDONOVSKI, *USA head coach*

FACTS AND FIGURES

BORN: 2 JULY 1989
POSITION: FORWARD
CLUBS: WESTERN NEW YORK FLASH (USA), SEATTLE SOUNDERS (USA), PORTLAND THORNS (USA), ORLANDO PRIDE (USA), OLYMPIQUE LYONNAIS (FRA), TOTTENHAM HOTSPUR (ENG), SAN DIEGO WAVE FC (USA)
CAPS/GOALS: 200/119

< 111 >

LENA OBERDORF

As last year's fourth-place *Ballon d'Or féminin* ranking confirmed, Lena Oberdorf is already rated as one of the world's best players. She will be a key player for Germany in this FIFA Women's World Cup.

FACTS AND FIGURES

BORN: 19 DECEMBER 2001
POSITION: MIDFIELDER
CLUBS: SGS ESSEN (GER), VFL WOLFSBURG (GER)
CAPS/GOALS: 35/3

Tough tackling "Obi" loves a one-on-one battle, but there is more to her game than breaking up attacks. Once in possession, this intelligent Gevelsberg native can use the ball to devastating effect.

She did so as *Die Nationalelf* took the 2022 UEFA Women's EURO by storm, the then-20-year-old performing like a seasoned veteran in the final even though it was only her 32nd cap.

Hailed by Germany coach Martina Voss-Tecklenburg for the maturity and sheer joy of her play, it came as little surprise to see the midfielder make the team of the tournament while also coming away as its best young player.

It was a big-stage success foretold at France 2019 when, aged just 17, Oberdorf broke Germany legend Birgit Prinz's record by 52 days to become the youngest player to represent Germany on the world stage.

She would play with a confidence that belied her years in four matches during that FIFA Women's World Cup, including their quarter-final defeat to Sweden.

It was not entirely unexpected. Aged 15, Oberdorf won the UEFA Women's U-17 Championship and was crowned player of the tournament, and at 16 had debuted in the *Frauen-Bundesliga* with SGS Essen.

What was remarkable, though, was the fact that she was still a schoolgirl. She was in lessons when Voss-Tecklenburg rang to say she had made the cut for France 2019 and even went on to sit exams during the tournament, including one two days before her competition debut.

As for her football education, that had started as a young child with her brother Tim, who now also plays professionally, her sister and parents all kicking about in the garden until it was too dark to see the ball.

Then came club football and competing alongside boys at TuS Ennepetal and TSG Sprockhövel, all experiences that added an aggressive, battling edge to her game.

A self-confessed Dzsenifer Marozsán admirer, who as a child once asked another Germany star, Alexandra Popp, for her autograph, Oberdorf is a DFB-Frauen fans' favourite herself these days.

Another solid performance at this, her third major tournament, will only serve to enhance her standing across the globe.

> "You forget she's still so young because she plays with such maturity. She's a real animal and so important for the team. When she has the ball, she has a calmness and assuredness about her."

SARA DÄBRITZ, *Germany midfielder*

< 112 >

ASISAT OSHOALA

A title winner on three continents who boasts a raft of unique personal accolades, Asisat Oshoala is more than a talismanic figure in Nigeria: she is their women's football GOAT.

Asisat Oshoala's list of "firsts" as an African woman is phenomenal. With Liverpool in 2015, she became the first to play in England's top flight; at Barcelona six years later, the first to win the UEFA Women's Champions League.

In 2022, after a treble-winning but injury-hit season, "Super Zee" broke the mould again as the first African woman to claim the Spanish *Pichichi* top scorer prize, going on to receive a prestigious *Ballon d'Or féminin* nomination.

It is all a far cry from the days when she would defy her parents to play football for fun on the streets of Lagos. Her schoolgirl dream was to become a lawyer, but her teenage focus turned to football after meeting FC Robo founding coach Emmanuel Osahon Orobosa.

Wowed by Oshoala's height and speed, Osahon convinced her parents to let her play and kick-started a football education that would lead to title wins and international call-ups.

Her big break came in 2014 when, playing with freedom and joy in the green and white of Nigeria, she bossed the FIFA U-20 Women's World Cup, winning the Golden Ball and Boot as well as a runners-up medal.

Another best player award followed with the seniors on the way to her first continental title and she closed out the year as a league and cup double winner with Rivers Angels, and as Africa's Women's Player and Youth Player of the Year.

In 2015, she left Nigeria to begin an overseas odyssey that continues today. Highlights include an FA Cup win with Arsenal and multiple title tilts in China PR at Dalian Quanjian and at Barcelona too.

There were moments when she wondered if she had made the right choices, but these days her proud parents are her biggest fans and she helps girl footballers in Nigeria combine education with sport through her own foundation and academy.

Perhaps the one success that eludes this five-time African Women's Player of the Year is with Nigeria at the FIFA Women's World Cup. Oshoala has already targeted bettering 2019's run to the round of 16. This fast, powerful and instinctive 28-year-old forward will spearhead the *Super Falcons* attack, and play her heart out to achieve it.

"When you see the kind of spirit she brings into the game, it wakes every other player up. She wants to be the best."

ONOME EBI, *veteran Nigeria defender*

< 113 >

ALEXIA PUTELLAS

La Roja's most-capped player and inspirational captain is attacking midfielder Alexia Putellas. Both a star and devoted fan of Barcelona, she has established herself as the outstanding female footballer of the 2020s.

FACTS AND FIGURES

BORN: 4 FEBRUARY 1994
POSITION: MIDFIELDER
CLUBS: RCD ESPANYOL (ESP), LEVANTE UD (ESP), FC BARCELONA (ESP)
CAPS/GOALS: 100/27

Following the world-record crowds at Barcelona's Camp Nou in spring 2022, a mural appeared on a wall in the city featuring Alexia Putellas depicted in a *Blaugranes*-style superhero outfit, with the accompanying message "Follow Your Dreams".

Of course, the first player to win the *Ballon d'Or féminin* and UEFA Women's Player of the Year award twice in a row, in 2021 and 2022, is doing just that.

Putellas is a left-footed playmaker, great dribbler and striker of the ball, physically strong and good in the air. She has the gift that truly special players possess – the ability to carry a team to victory.

The first Spanish woman to reach 100 caps for her country, her career ascent is born from total dedication as well as supreme natural talent. The former was vital to recovering from the major knee injury she suffered on the eve of the 2022 UEFA Women's EURO, which could have proved devastating.

"I never imagined I'd reach this level," she said when crowned The Best FIFA Women's Player in 2021. "But when you put in the work and people have faith in you, the results come. That's how it has been for me."

Born in Mollet del Vallès and from a Barça-mad family, she joined Sabadell aged seven and competed with the older girls. After a season at Barcelona's youth academy, five years at Espanyol and another with Levante, she returned to her beloved club aged 18 in 2012, and together they have achieved dominance.

Putellas was the first female Barça player to score at the Camp Nou and has been pivotal in six league titles, seven Copa de la Reina wins, two Spanish Super Cups, seven Copa Catalunya triumphs and three UEFA Women's Champions League final appearances, lifting the coveted trophy in 2021. Though Barça were only runners-up in 2021-22, she was still top scorer with 11 goals and named player of the tournament.

Her status is helping elevate the women's game as a whole, with a series of *Alexia Superfutbolista* children's books, and she is the highest-rated player, irrespective of gender, in the video game *FIFA 23*.

> "She is passionate about football and understands it very well, which is not something every player has. She has so much quality, sees things before others and executes everything with pace and style."
>
> JORGE VILDA, *Spain head coach*

< 114 >

WANG SHUANG

Wang Shuang is a magically creative, left-footed midfielder and regarded as China PR's "once in a generation" talent. She has been her country's women's footballer of the year four times.

FACTS AND FIGURES

BORN: 23 JANUARY 1995
POSITION: MIDFIELDER
CLUBS: WUHAN JIANGDA (CHN), SPORTSTOTO (KOR), DALIAN QUANJIAN (CHN), PARIS SAINT-GERMAIN (FRA), RACING LOUISVILLE (USA)
CAPS/GOALS: 116/39

A mazy dribbler and set-piece specialist, Wang Shuang's admirers refer to her as "Lady Messi". When her team-mates and national team coach Shui Qingxia talk about her, they use words like "courageous" and "confident".

The first Chinese player to score in the UEFA Women's Champions League has always had the ability, but it took time for her to develop self-belief.

Sent to Beijing to study and play at the age of 12, later that year she was selected for the U-17 national team. By 15, she was playing in the U-20s and featured at the FIFA U-20 Women's World Cup aged 17.

In 2013, Wang made her senior debut for China PR against Canada at the Four Nations Tournament in Yongchuan, 11 days before her 18th birthday.

She was substituted on in the 57th minute, but was overawed and taken off again 27 minutes later. Even so, she persevered and six years later made her 100th appearance for China PR in the very same stadium.

After a confidence-boosting season for Korean side Sportstoto, she went on to enjoy back-to-back Chinese Women's Super League titles with now-defunct club Dalian Quanjian.

A move to French giants Paris Saint-Germain yielded eight goals in 27 appearances across all competitions; over 8 million fans followed a mini-series about her time in Paris on social media.

Winner of two successive league titles with her hometown club Wuhan Jiangda in 2020 and 2021, the first was attained, remarkably, following the COVID-19-enforced two-month lockdown in the city. Wang personally donated 600,000 Yuan to Wuhan's frontline medical workers. She started a new adventure at Racing Louisville in the USA last summer.

It is for her star turns with China PR that this playmaker is best known in her homeland, though.

Wang has dominated the player of the year accolade since 2017. She scored six on the way to silver at the 2018 Asian Games, played in all four matches at France 2019, and her goals were crucial in qualifying for the Tokyo Olympics.

Last year, she joint top-scored for China PR with five in the 2022 AFC Women's Asian Cup, playing through pain in the final to help them claim their record-extending ninth continental title.

"Wang is a game changer — a player who can do a little bit extra for your team. She can look to the left and surprise everyone with a pass to the right. Her left foot is top quality and she's always dangerous on set pieces."

KIM BJÖRKEGREN, *head coach of Racing Louisville*

< 115 >

FIFA WOMEN'S WORLD CUP RECORDS

* * *

The FIFA Women's World Cup may be relatively young compared to the men's competition, but records have been set since the very first match was played in Guangzhou, China PR back in 1991, with many smashed as the various editions have gone by. From the most successful teams, to top-scoring players, biggest wins, momentous golden goals and awe-inspiring attendances, these statistics, fun facts and remarkable feats all make for fascinating reading.

FIFA WOMEN'S WORLD CUP TEAM RECORDS

Football is a team game and teamwork makes the dream work. With plenty of silverware at stake, many nations have made their mark on the biggest stage but some more than others.

FIFA WOMEN'S WORLD CUP MEDAL MATCHES

Year	Host	Final			Match for third place		
1991	China PR	USA	2-1	Norway	Sweden	4-0	Germany
1995	Sweden	Norway	2-0	Germany	USA	2-0	China PR
1999	USA	USA	0-0 AET 5-4 pens	China PR	Brazil	0-0 AET 5-4 pens	Norway
2003	USA	Germany	2-1 AET	Sweden	USA	3-1	Canada
2007	China PR	Germany	2-0	Brazil	USA	4-1	Norway
2011	Germany	Japan	2-2 AET 3-1 pens	USA	Sweden	2-1	France
2015	Canada	USA	5-2	Japan	England	1-0 AET	Germany
2019	France	USA	2-0	Netherlands	Sweden	2-1	England

MOST FIFA WOMEN'S WORLD CUP FINAL APPEARANCES

5 USA	1 Brazil
3 Germany	1 China PR
2 Japan	1 Netherlands
2 Norway	1 Sweden

MOST FIFA WOMEN'S WORLD CUP FINAL VICTORIES

4 USA
2 Germany
1 Japan
1 Norway

MOST FIFA WOMEN'S WORLD CUP RUNNERS-UP FINISHES

1 Brazil	1 Netherlands
1 China PR	1 Norway
1 Germany	1 Sweden
1 Japan	1 USA

MOST FIFA WOMEN'S WORLD CUP THIRD-PLACE FINISHES

3 Sweden
3 USA
1 Brazil
1 England

ABOVE: Germany retained their title at the FIFA Women's World Cup 2007.

< 118 >

FIFA WOMEN'S WORLD CUP ALL-TIME RANKING TOP TEN

Rank	Team	Tournaments played	Matches played	Won	Drawn	Lost	Goals scored	Goals conceded	Goal difference
1	USA	8	50	40	6	4	138	38	+100
2	Germany	8	44	30	5	9	121	39	+82
3	Norway	8	40	24	4	12	93	52	+41
4	Sweden	8	40	23	5	12	71	48	+23
5	Brazil	8	34	20	4	10	66	40	+26
6	China PR	7	33	16	7	10	53	32	+21
7	England	5	26	15	4	7	43	30	+13
8	Japan	8	33	14	4	15	39	59	-20
9	France	4	19	10	3	6	32	20	+12
10	Canada	7	27	8	5	14	34	52	-18

FIFA WOMEN'S WORLD CUP EVER-PRESENT TEAMS 1991–2023

Africa	Asia	Europe	North America	South America
Nigeria	Japan	Germany, Norway, Sweden	USA	Brazil

BEST FINISHERS

USA have never finished outside of the top 3.

Germany have never finished outside of the top 8.

HOSTS AND CHAMPIONS

USA are the only hosts to make it past the quarter-finals, in 1999 and 2003.

Japan are the only champions to have lost a match on the way to the final, in 2011.

GROUP RECORDS

Most goals scored in the group stage
= 18, USA (France 2019)

Most goals conceded in the group stage
= 20, Thailand (France 2019)

DID YOU KNOW...?

In their record-breaking run to the 2019 title, champions USA went two better than Germany's previous record of 15 unbeaten FIFA Women's World Cup matches and surpassed Norway's long-standing winning-run record when they beat the Netherlands in the final, their 12th victory on the bounce.

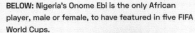

BELOW: Nigeria's Onome Ebi is the only African player, male or female, to have featured in five FIFA World Cups.

ABOVE: USA celebrate winning the FIFA Women's World Cup in 2019, their fourth success.

< 119 >

FIFA WOMEN'S WORLD CUP PLAYER RECORDS

Every four years, legends are made. While some players' achievements span multiple tournaments, others find themselves in the annals after just one moment. All have their place in the FIFA Women's World Cup story.

MOST FIFA WOMEN'S WORLD CUP TOURNAMENTS
7 Formiga (BRA) 1995-2019
6 Homare Sawa (JPN) 1995-2015

MOST FIFA WOMEN'S WORLD CUP APPEARANCES
30 Kristine Lilly (USA) 1991-2007
27 Formiga (BRA) 1995-2019
25 Carli Lloyd (USA) 2007-2019
25 Abby Wambach (USA) 2003-2015

MOST FIFA WOMEN'S WORLD CUP FINAL APPEARANCES
3 Birgit Prinz (GER); Tobin Heath, Ali Krieger, Carli Lloyd, Alex Morgan and Megan Rapinoe (USA)

ABOVE: The USA's Kristine Lilly has made the most appearances at the competition.

YOUNGEST AND OLDEST AT THE FIFA WOMEN'S WORLD CUP
Youngest player to play in the FIFA Women's World Cup final:
  Birgit Prinz (GER), aged 17y/236d in 1995
Oldest player to play in the FIFA Women's World Cup final:
  Christie Rampone (USA), aged 40y/11d in 2015
Youngest player to play at the FIFA Women's World Cup:
  Ifeanyi Chiejine (NGA), aged 16y/34d in 1999
Oldest player to play at the FIFA Women's World Cup:
  Formiga (BRA), aged 41y/112d in 2019
Youngest player to score at the FIFA Women's World Cup:
  Elena Danilova (RUS), aged 16y/107d in 2003
Oldest player to score at the FIFA Women's World Cup:
  Formiga (BRA), aged 37y/98d in 2015
Oldest player to score a brace at the FIFA Women's World Cup:
  Carli Lloyd (USA), aged 36y/335d in 2019
Oldest player to score a hat-trick at the FIFA Women's World Cup:
  Cristiane (BRA), aged 34y/25d in 2019

LEFT: Brazilian midfield legend Formiga played at seven FIFA Women's World Cups.

< 120 >

FIFA WOMEN'S WORLD CUP BEST PLAYER AWARDS

Year	Golden Ball	Silver Ball	Bronze Ball
1991	Carin Jennings (USA)	Michelle Akers (USA)	Linda Medalen (NOR)
1995	Hege Riise (NOR)	Gro Espeseth (NOR)	Ann Kristin Aarønes (NOR)
1999	Sun Wen (CHN)	Sissi (BRA)	Michelle Akers (USA)
2003	Birgit Prinz (GER)	Victoria Svensson (SWE)	Maren Meinert (GER)
2007	Marta (BRA)	Birgit Prinz (GER)	Cristiane (BRA)
2011	Homare Sawa (JPN)	Abby Wambach (USA)	Hope Solo (USA)
2015	Carli Lloyd (USA)	Amandine Henry (FRA)	Aya Miyama (JPN)
2019	Megan Rapinoe (USA)	Lucy Bronze (ENG)	Rose Lavelle (USA)

FIFA WOMEN'S WORLD CUP YOUNG PLAYER AWARD

Year	Golden Ball
2011	Caitlin Foord (AUS)
2015	Kadeisha Buchanan (CAN)
2019	Giulia Gwinn (GER)

FIFA WOMEN'S WORLD CUP GOLDEN GLOVE AWARD

Year	Golden Glove
2003	Silke Rottenberg (GER)
2007	Nadine Angerer (GER)
2011	Hope Solo (USA)
2015	Hope Solo (USA)
2019	Sari van Veenendaal (NED)

DID YOU KNOW...?

Alex Morgan was the first player to score on her birthday at the FIFA Women's World Cup when she netted the winning goal in the semi-final against England at France 2019, the very day she turned 30.

ABOVE: The USA's Hope Solo is a two-time winner of the Golden Glove award.

RIGHT: Japan captain Homare Sawa with her best player and top scorer awards after winning the FIFA Women's World Cup 2011.

< 121 >

FIFA WOMEN'S WORLD CUP GOALSCORING RECORDS

The previous edition of the FIFA Women's World Cup served up goals galore but how does that compare with earlier tournaments and who do we have to thank for all the memorable moments?

TOP-SCORING TEAM AT EACH FIFA WOMEN'S WORLD CUP

Year	Team	Goals
1991	USA	25
1995	Norway	23
1999	China PR	19
2003	Germany	25
2007	Germany	21
2011	USA	13
2015	Germany	20
2019	USA	26

GOLDEN BOOT AT EACH FIFA WOMEN'S WORLD CUP

Year	Winner	Goals
1991	Michelle Akers (USA)	10
1995	Ann Kristin Aarønes (NOR)	6
1999	Sissi (BRA); Sun Wen (CHN)	7
2003	Birgit Prinz (GER)	7
2007	Marta (BRA)	7
2011	Homare Sawa (JPN)	5
2015	Celia Šašić (GER)	6
2019	Megan Rapinoe (USA)	6

TOTAL GOALS AT EACH FIFA WOMEN'S WORLD CUP

Year	Total goals	No. of matches	Average per match
1991	99	26	3.81
1995	99	26	3.81
1999	123	32	3.84
2003	107	32	3.34
2007	111	32	3.47
2011	86	32	2.69
2015	146	52	2.81
2019	146	52	2.81

RIGHT: FIFA's joint-Women's Player of the Century Michelle Akers holds her top scorer trophy after bagging ten goals in the FIFA Women's World Cup 1991.

FIFA WOMEN'S WORLD CUP ALL-TIME LEADING GOALSCORERS

Player	Goals	Tournaments scored in (and played in)
Marta (BRA)	17	2003, 2007, 2011, 2015, 2019
Birgit Prinz (GER)	14	1995, 1999, 2003, 2007, (2011)
Abby Wambach (USA)	14	2003, 2007, 2011, 2015
Michelle Akers (USA)	12	1991, (1995), 1999
Cristiane (BRA)	11	(2003), 2007, 2011, (2015), 2019
Sun Wen (CHN)	11	1991, 1995, 1999, 2003
Bettina Wiegmann (GER)	11	1991, 1995, 1999, 2003

< 122 >

FIFA WOMEN'S WORLD CUP MOST GOALS IN A SINGLE MATCH

5 Michelle Akers, USA 7-0 Chinese Taipei, China PR 1991
5 Alex Morgan, USA 13-0 Thailand, France 2019
4 Sam Kerr, Australia 4-1 Jamaica, France 2019

FIFA WOMEN'S WORLD CUP HIGHEST-SCORING MATCHES

USA 13-0 Thailand, France 2019
Germany 11-0 Argentina, China PR 2007
Switzerland 10-1 Ecuador, Canada 2015
Germany 10-0 Côte d'Ivoire, Canada 2015
Norway 7-2 Ghana, China PR 2007

BEST SCORING RUNS AT THE FIFA WOMEN'S WORLD CUP

6 consecutive matches: Carli Lloyd (USA) 2015-2019
5 consecutive matches: Linda Medalen (NOR) 1991-95,
   Heidi Mohr (GER) 1991, Birgit Prinz (GER) 2003

MILESTONE GOALS IN THE FIFA WOMEN'S WORLD CUP

1st goal	Ma Li, China PR 4-0 Norway in 1991
100th goal	Silvia Neid, Germany 1-0 Japan in 1995
200th goal	Julie Foudy, USA 3-0 Denmark in 1999
300th goal	Marianne Pettersen, Norway 3-1 Sweden in 1999
400th goal	Alberta Sackey, Ghana 2-1 Australia in 2003
500th goal	Ragnhild Gulbrandsen, Norway 7-2 Ghana in 2007
600th goal	Jill Scott, England 1-1 France in 2011
700th goal	Melanie Leupolz, Germany 4-0 Thailand in 2015
800th goal	Samantha Mewis, USA 13-0 Thailand in 2019
900th goal	Lucy Bronze, England 3-0 Norway in 2019

DID YOU KNOW...?

The first player to score in five editions of the FIFA Women's World Cup, Brazil's Marta, buried two penalties at France 2019, bringing her spot-kick haul up to seven; only Bettina Wiegmann of Germany has scored more, with eight. Within days, Christine Sinclair of Canada had repeated the feat of netting in five consecutive finals, becoming the eleventh player to hit double figures to boot.

BELOW: Brazil's Marta netted two penalties in 2019 to extend her lead as the FIFA Women's World Cup all-time top scorer.

ABOVE: Hosts China PR prior to the FIFA Women's World Cup 1991 opener against Norway.

< 123 >

OTHER FIFA WOMEN'S WORLD CUP RECORDS

Those big numbers are there for all to see; as the tournament grows in stature, so do the figures. But let's not forget the people who help make it happen — the coaches and referees who let the players shine.

FIFA WOMEN'S WORLD CUP VENUES, TEAMS AND MATCHES

Year	Host	No. of venues	No. of teams	No. of matches
1991	China PR	6	12	26
1995	Sweden	5	12	26
1999	USA	8	16	32
2003	USA	6	16	32
2007	China PR	5	16	32
2011	Germany	9	16	32
2015	Canada	6	24	52
2019	France	9	24	52

ABOVE: A record crowd of 90,185 attended the Rose Bowl for the FIFA Women's World Cup 1999 final.

FIFA WOMEN'S WORLD CUP OPENING MATCHES

Date	Host	Venue and city	Result	Attendance
16 Nov 1991	China PR	Tianhe Stadium, Guangzhou	China PR 4-0 Norway	65,000
5 Jun 1995	Sweden	Olympia Stadium, Helsingborg	Sweden 0-1 Brazil	14,500
19 Jun 1999	USA	Giants Stadium, New York/New Jersey	USA 3-0 Denmark	78,972
20 Sep 2003	USA	Lincoln Financial Field, Philadelphia	Norway 2-0 France	24,346
10 Sep 2007	China PR	Shanghai Hongkou Football Stadium, Shanghai	Germany 11-0 Argentina	28,098
26 Jun 2011	Germany	Olympiastadion, Berlin	Germany 2-1 Canada	73,680
6 Jun 2015	Canada	Commonwealth Stadium, Edmonton	Canada 1-0 China PR	53,058
7 Jun 2019	France	Parc des Princes, Paris	France 4-0 Korea Republic	45,261

FIFA WOMEN'S WORLD CUP FINALS

Date	Host	Venue and city	Result	Attendance
30 Nov 1991	China PR	Tianhe Stadium, Guangzhou	USA 2-1 Norway	63,000
18 Jun 1995	Sweden	Råsunda Stadium, Solna	Norway 2-0 Germany	17,158
10 Jul 1999	USA	Rose Bowl, Pasadena	USA 0-0 China PR (5-4 on pens)	90,185
12 Oct 2003	USA	Home Depot Center, Carson	Germany 2-1 Sweden	26,137
30 Sep 2007	China PR	Shanghai Hongkou Football Stadium, Shanghai	Germany 2-0 Brazil	31,000
17 Jul 2011	Germany	FIFA Women's World Cup Stadium, Frankfurt	Japan 2-2 USA (3-1 on pens)	48,817
5 Jul 2015	Canada	BC Place Stadium, Vancouver	USA 5-2 Japan	53,341
7 Jul 2019	France	Stade de Lyon, Lyon	USA 2-0 Netherlands	57,900

< 124 >

FIFA WOMEN'S WORLD CUP TOURNAMENT ATTENDANCES

Year	Total attendance	Average per match
1991	510,000	19,615
1995	112,213	4,316
1999	1,214,221	37,944
2003	679,664	21,240
2007	1,190,971	37,218
2011	845,711	26,428
2015	1,353,506	26,029
2019	1,131,312	21,756

FIFA WOMEN'S WORLD CUP FINAL REFEREES

Year	Referee	Final
1991	Vadim Zhuk (BLR)	USA 2-1 Norway
1995	Ingrid Jonsson (SWE)	Norway 2-0 Germany
1999	Nicole Petignat (SUI)	USA 0-0 China PR
2003	Floarea Cristina Ionescu (ROU)	Germany 2-1 Sweden
2007	Tammy Ogston (AUS)	Germany 2-0 Brazil
2011	Bibiana Steinhaus (GER)	Japan 2-2 USA
2015	Kateryna Monzul (UKR)	USA 5-2 Japan
2019	Stéphanie Frappart (FRA)	USA 2-0 Netherlands

FIFA WOMEN'S WORLD CUP-WINNING COACHES

Year	Coach	Team
1991	Anson Dorrance	USA
1995	Even Pellerud	Norway
1999	Tony DiCicco	USA
2003	Tina Theune-Meyer	Germany
2007	Silvia Neid	Germany
2011	Norio Sasaki	Japan
2015	Jill Ellis	USA
2019	Jill Ellis	USA

ABOVE: Stéphanie Frappart (second from left), referee for the FIFA Women's World Cup 2019 final.

MOST EXPERENCED FIFA WOMEN'S WORLD CUP COACHES

25 matches, Even Pellerud (NOR) at 5 tournaments
(NOR 1991-1995; CAN 2003-2007; NOR 2015)

17 matches, Silvia Neid (GER) at 3 tournaments
(GER 2007-2015)

14 matches, Marika Domanski Lyfors (SWE) at 3 tournaments
(SWE 1999-2003; CHN 2007)

14 matches, Jill Ellis (USA) at 2 tournaments (USA 2015-2019)

14 matches, Tom Sermanni (SCO) at 4 tournaments
(AUS 1995/2007/2011; NZL 2019)

13 matches, Thomas Dennerby (SWE) at 3 tournaments
(SWE 2007-2011; NGA 2019)

13 matches, Norio Sasaki (JPN) at 2 tournaments (JPN 2011-2015)

DID YOU KNOW...?

The golden goal era may have been fairly contentious and brief but it lives long in the memory when it comes to the FIFA Women's World Cup. After a stunning fight-back from Nigeria in the 1999 quarter-final was finally snuffed out by an inch-perfect Sissi extra-time free kick, the second and final golden goal decided the 2003 world champions, Sweden succumbing to a Germany sucker punch yet again after losing the EURO final in the same manner just two years previously.

LEFT: Even Pellerud of Norway and Germany's Silvia Neid at the FIFA Women's World Cup 2015 – between them they have overseen 42 matches at the finals.

MATCH SCHEDULE

🕐 **All match times are local and subject to change.**
Australian Western Standard Time (AWST) is UTC +8; Australian Central Standard Time (ACST) is UTC +9.5; Australian Eastern Standard Time (AEST) is UTC +10; New Zealand Standard Time (NZST) is UTC +12.

GROUP A

Date	Time	Team 1		Team 2	Venue
20 Jul	19:00	New Zealand		Norway	Auckland
21 Jul	17:00	Philippines		Switzerland	Dunedin
25 Jul	17:30	New Zealand		Philippines	Wellington
25 Jul	20:00	Switzerland		Norway	Hamilton
30 Jul	19:00	Switzerland		New Zealand	Dunedin
30 Jul	19:00	Norway		Philippines	Auckland

Team	P	W	D	L	GD	Pts

GROUP B

Date	Time	Team 1		Team 2	Venue
20 Jul	20:00	Australia		Rep. of Ireland	Sydney
21 Jul	12:30	Nigeria		Canada	Melbourne
26 Jul	20:00	Canada		Rep. of Ireland	Perth
27 Jul	20:00	Australia		Nigeria	Brisbane
31 Jul	20:00	Canada		Australia	Melbourne
31 Jul	20:00	Rep. of Ireland		Nigeria	Brisbane

Team	P	W	D	L	GD	Pts

GROUP C

Date	Time	Team 1		Team 2	Venue
21 Jul	19:30	Spain		Costa Rica	Wellington
22 Jul	19:00	Zambia		Japan	Hamilton
26 Jul	17:00	Japan		Costa Rica	Dunedin
26 Jul	19:30	Spain		Zambia	Auckland
31 Jul	19:00	Japan		Spain	Wellington
31 Jul	19:00	Costa Rica		Zambia	Hamilton

Team	P	W	D	L	GD	Pts

GROUP D

Date	Time	Team 1		Team 2	Venue
22 Jul	19:30	England		Play-Off B	Brisbane
22 Jul	20:00	Denmark		China PR	Perth
28 Jul	18:30	England		Denmark	Sydney
28 Jul	20:30	China PR		Play-Off B	Adelaide
1 Aug	20:30	China PR		England	Adelaide
1 Aug	19:00	Play-Off B		Denmark	Perth

Team	P	W	D	L	GD	Pts

GROUP E

Date	Time	Team 1		Team 2	Venue
22 Jul	13:00	USA		Vietnam	Auckland
23 Jul	19:30	Netherlands		Play-Off A	Dunedin
27 Jul	13:00	USA		Netherlands	Wellington
27 Jul	19:30	Play-Off A		Vietnam	Hamilton
1 Aug	19:00	Play-Off A		USA	Auckland
1 Aug	19:00	Vietnam		Netherlands	Dunedin

Team	P	W	D	L	GD	Pts

GROUP F

Date	Time	Team 1		Team 2	Venue
23 Jul	20:00	France		Jamaica	Sydney
24 Jul	20:30	Brazil		Play-Off C	Adelaide
29 Jul	20:00	France		Brazil	Brisbane
29 Jul	20:30	Play-Off C		Jamaica	Perth
2 Aug	20:00	Play-Off C		France	Sydney
2 Aug	20:00	Jamaica		Brazil	Melbourne

Team	P	W	D	L	GD	Pts

< 126 >

GROUP G

23 Jul, 17:00	Sweden	⚪⚪	South Africa	Wellington
24 Jul, 18:00	Italy	⚪⚪	Argentina	Auckland
28 Jul, 12:00	Argentina	⚪⚪	South Africa	Dunedin
29 Jul, 19:30	Sweden	⚪⚪	Italy	Wellington
2 Aug, 19:00	Argentina	⚪⚪	Sweden	Hamilton
2 Aug, 19:00	South Africa	⚪⚪	Italy	Wellington

Team	P	W	D	L	GD	Pts

GROUP H

24 Jul, 18:30	Germany	Morocco	Melbourne
25 Jul, 12:00	Colombia	Korea Rep.	Sydney
30 Jul, 14:00	Korea Rep.	Morocco	Adelaide
30 Jul, 19:30	Germany	Colombia	Sydney
3 Aug, 20:00	Korea Rep.	Germany	Brisbane
3 Aug, 18:00	Morocco	Colombia	Perth

Team	P	W	D	L	GD	Pts

ROUND OF 16

5 Aug, 17:00	Winner A	⚪ ⚪	Runner-up C	Auckland
5 Aug, 20:00	Winner C	⚪ ⚪	Runner-up A	Wellington
6 Aug, 12:00	Winner E	⚪ ⚪	Runner-up G	Sydney
6 Aug, 19:00	Winner G	⚪ ⚪	Runner-up E	Melbourne
7 Aug, 17:30	Winner D	⚪ ⚪	Runner-up B	Brisbane
7 Aug, 20:30	Winner B	⚪ ⚪	Runner-up D	Sydney
8 Aug, 18:00	Winner H	⚪ ⚪	Runner-up F	Melbourne
8 Aug, 20:30	Winner F	⚪ ⚪	Runner-up H	Adelaide

QUARTER-FINALS

11 Aug, 13:00	Winner 1	⚪ ⚪	Winner 3	Wellington
11 Aug, 19:30	Winner 2	⚪ ⚪	Winner 4	Auckland
12 Aug, 17:00	Winner 5	⚪ ⚪	Winner 7	Brisbane
12 Aug, 20:30	Winner 6	⚪ ⚪	Winner 8	Sydney

SEMI-FINALS

| 15 Aug, 20:00 | Winner QF1 | ⚪ ⚪ | Winner QF2 | Auckland |
| 16 Aug, 20:00 | Winner QF3 | ⚪ ⚪ | Winner QF4 | Sydney |

THIRD-PLACE PLAY-OFF

| 19 Aug, 18:00 | Loser SF1 | ⚪ ⚪ | Loser SF2 | Brisbane |

FINAL

| 20 Aug, 20:00 | Winner SF1 | ⚪ ⚪ | Winner SF2 | Sydney |

< 127 >

CREDITS

AUTHORS' ACKNOWLEDGEMENTS:

Thanks to the following association and confederation websites for quotes used: afa.com.
ar; cafonline.com; canadasoccer.com; concacaf.com; dbu.dk; dfb.de; FIFA.com; FIFA+; fff.fr;
figc.it; fotball.no; jfa.jp; knvb.nl; matildas.com.au; uefa.com; ussoccer.com. And our gratitude
also goes to the following reporters and websites for permission to use quotes: Agustin
Fernandez of aucklandcityfc.com; Martín Feijóo; Om Arvind and @ElPatiofutbolfemenino;
Jeroen van Barneveld (sports writer http://NU.nl); L'Équipière.com; Jonathan Lintner and
Racing Lousville; Ameé Ruszkai. Thanks also to AS FAR and Dietmar Ness.